Legislative Analysis and Drafting

Second Edition

Legislative Analysis and Drafting

Second Edition

William P. Statsky

Editors

John F. O'Connell
Professor of Law
Western State University College of Law

Bruce Comly French
Legislative Counsel, Council of the District of Columbia
Associate Member, National Conference of Commissioners
  on Uniform State Laws

West Publishing Company
St. Paul   New York   Los Angeles   San Francisco

Library of Congress Cataloging in Publication Data

Statsky, William P.
 Legislative analysis and drafting.

 Bibliography: p.
 Includes index.
 1. Law—United States—Interpretation and construction.
 2. Bill drafting—United States. I. Title.
 KF425.S79 1984   349.73   83–19854
 ISBN 0–314–77815–2   347.3

For

Jessica Statsky
Wilhelmina K. S.,
and Acissej

Also by William P. Statsky

Case Analysis and Fundamentals of Legal Writing, 2d ed., St. Paul: West Publishing Company, 1984 (with J. Wernet)

Legal Research, Writing and Analysis, 2d ed., St. Paul: West Publishing Company, 1982

Torts: Personal Injury Litigation, St. Paul: West Publishing Company, 1982

Contents

Legislative Analysis and Drafting

Second Edition

Chapter One

The Role of the
Courts in the
Interpretation of Statutes

Section A. Introduction to Legislative Analysis

By January 1913, F. Drew Caminetti was a man of some prominence in Sacramento, California. He was married and had one child. In that month he began dating Lola Norris, a single woman who lived with her parents. They took long rides (in his "machine") outside the city, where they spent the nights together at hotels, falsely registering as husband and wife.

Soon their relationship became a scandal in the community. A local newspaper, the Sacramento Bee, was about to run a story on their affair. Panic-stricken, Drew decided to leave the state with Lola. He arranged for the purchase of tickets on the Southern Pacific Railroad to Reno, Nevada, where they planned to live together. On the trip to Reno they occupied the same bed in the drawing room of a Pullman car. In Reno they rented a cottage, again claiming to be husband and wife. Several days later F. Drew Caminetti was arrested on a charge of violating the White Slave Traffic

Act, a criminal statute enacted by Congress. The indictment against Caminetti alleged that he

> did willfully, unlawfully, and feloniously knowingly persuade, induce, and entice, and cause to be persuaded, induced, and enticed, and aid and assist in persuading, inducing, and enticing, Lola Norris to go from the city of Sacramento, Cal., to Reno, Nev., in interstate commerce over the line of railroad of the Southern Pacific Company, a common carrier of passengers between the points named, for the purpose of debauchery and for an immoral purpose, to wit, that she, the Lola Norris, should be and become the concubine and mistress of the said defendant.

The criminal trial in California caused considerable notoriety. Counsel for the prosecution told the jury that the eyes of "60,000,000 or 90,000,000 people are awaiting your verdict in this case. . . . Gentlemen, if there is any depraved man in the world . . . it is that man . . . who seduces an innocent girl and exposes her shame to the world. . . . [T]he government demands that the laws enacted for the protection and preservation of its young and decent women be adequately and rigorously enforced. An acquittal in this case would be a miscarriage of justice, and it would be a blot upon the fair name and escutcheon of California."

To many there seemed little doubt that Caminetti would be convicted. The criminal statute he was charged with violating provided

> That any person who shall knowingly transport or cause to be transported . . . in interstate or foreign commerce, . . . any woman or girl for the purpose of prostitution or debauchery, or for any other immoral purpose, . . . shall be deemed guilty of a felony, and upon conviction thereof shall be punished by a fine not exceeding five thousand dollars, or by an imprisonment of not more than five years, or by both. Comp.Stat.1913, § 8813

No one claimed that Caminetti had brought Norris across state lines to engage in prostitution. But who could doubt that he had an "immoral" purpose in making this trip? He was a married man sleeping with an unmarried woman. He engaged in this activity before, during, and after the trip. The statute was clear. If you examined the four corners of the face of the statute, the plain meaning of Congress in enacting it was evident. Three courts took this position. At the trial court a jury convicted Caminetti. He received a sentence of two years imprisonment and a fine of $2000. The Court of Appeals for the Ninth Circuit affirmed the conviction as did the U. S. Supreme Court. Caminetti v. United States, 242 U.S. 470, 37 S.Ct. 192, 61 L.Ed. 442 (1917).

But was the case this simple? Did the courts properly fulfill their role in applying a statute of the legislature? To this day many believe that they did not.

The guiding principle of the Supreme Court in affirming the conviction of Caminetti was the *plain meaning rule:*

> Where the language is plain and admits of no more than one meaning, the duty of interpretation does not arise, and the rules which are said to aid doubtful meanings need no discussion. There is no ambiguity in the terms of this act. 242 U.S. at 485.

Few would disagree with the premise that there is no need to spend a lot of time worrying about the meaning of that which is clear. Yet was the statute clear in this case? Is it true that there is "no more than one meaning" of the phrase "debauchery, or . . . any other immoral purpose"? Consider the following different meanings:

1. *any* debauchery or *any* other immoral purpose *or*
2. any *commercialized* debauchery or any other *commercialized* immoral purpose

Are *both* reasonable candidates for the meaning of the language in the statute? The question was crucial for Caminetti. While many would consider his conduct to be immoral, no one was charging him with trying to make a profit out of his conduct. There was no commercialized debauchery or immorality. Which meaning did Congress intend?

The prosecution successfully argued that Congress did not intend the second meaning. The statute says:

> prostitution *or* debauchery, *or* for any other immoral purpose. [emphasis added]

Commercialized debauchery and commercialized immorality are already covered by the word "prostitution." In the main, prostitution means sex and immorality for profit. Congress provided *additional* means of violating the statute which are *alternatives* to commercialized sex and immorality. Hence, whether Caminetti had a monetary or profit-making objective in transporting Norris across the state line is relevant only to a charge of prostitution. This objective does not have to be shown when the charge is debauchery or other immoral conduct. If this were not so, why did the legislature include these other categories of violations?

The defense, however, raised a number of compelling points. First, the name or title of the act, the White Slave Traffic Act, suggests that the statute was aimed at commercialized vice. The words "slave" and "traffic" refer to profit transactions or practices. Second, the legislative history of the statute indicated that the evil or mischief Congress was trying to rectify was the use of interstate commerce to pursue the *business* of vice. There was no intent to regulate every kind of immorality that involves crossing state lines. In the report of the committee of Congress that initially considered the statute, the following overview is provided:

> The White Slave Trade.—A material portion of the legislation suggested and proposed is necessary to meet conditions which have arisen in the last few years. The legislation is needed to put a stop to a villainous interstate and international traffic in women and girls. *The legislation is not needed or intended as an aid to the states in the exercise of their police powers in the suppression or regulation of immorality in general.* It does not attempt to regulate the practice of voluntary prostitution, but aims solely to prevent panderers and procurers from compelling thousands of women and girls against their will and desire to enter and continue in a life of prostitution. [emphasis added] H.R.Rep. No. 47, 61st Cong., 2d Sess. 9, 10.

While none of these arguments conclusively establish that the statute was intended to cover only commercialized prostitution, debauchery, and immorality (none of which could be connected with Caminetti), at the very least they establish that there is *some* doubt as to what Congress intended. The statute is not plain, unambiguous, and unamenable to more than one meaning.

The Supreme Court in 1917, however, took the position that there was nothing to interpret. Since the language of the statute was clear, there was no need to resort to any guidelines or rules of interpretation such as examining the title of the statute or its legislative history. It is true that no court will allow such guidelines or rules to alter the plain meaning of statutory language. But this begs the question of *whether* the language is plain and unambiguous. Shouldn't reliable guidance outside the four corners of the statute be used to determine *if* there is arguable ambiguity in the statute? Most courts today would answer this question in the affirmative, *including* the current Supreme Court. The approach taken in 1917 by the *Caminetti* Court is rarely followed today. We need to examine why this is so.

Assignment # 1

a. Assume that Caminetti was taking Norris to Nevada, where he planned to file for a divorce and then marry her. All the other facts remain the same. Has the statute been violated?

b. Assume that Caminetti is a photographer of nude women and that he took Norris to Nevada to take pictures of her for which she would be compensated. They had no personal relationship with each other in California or Nevada. Has the statute been violated?

c. Assume that Caminetti met Norris for the first time on the train to Nevada. While on the train, she seduced him. In Nevada, she became his mistress. Has the statute been violated?

Assignment # 2

To what extent do you think it would be proper in the original *Caminetti* case, or in any of the fact situations of Assignment # 1, for a trial court or an appellate court judge to call up a member of the legislature that wrote the statute (Congress) and ask for guidance on the meaning of the statute that was passed?

From the above discussion you can see that one of the main themes of legislative analysis is the somewhat delicate relationship between the courts and the legislature in our legal system. This book explores this theme through the following questions:

• What is the role of the courts in the application of statutes of the legislature?

• When is a court justified in going beyond the four corners of a statute in determining the meaning of the statute?

• What are the major rules or guidelines of statutory interpretation that can be used once it is determined that some assistance is needed?

Section B. Interpretation and the Judicial Role

There are two broad categories of law that preoccupy our courts: common law and enacted law.

1. COMMON LAW

Common law is judge-made law in the absence of controlling statutory law. Generally, if a case comes before a court which is not governed by any statutes because the legislature has never entered an area, the court will *create* law to fit the case. There is a rich variety of sources that a court relies on to create and develop common law: custom, tradition, maxims, morals, social policy, precedent in prior opinions, ancient statutes that are no longer on the books, etc. In a broad sense, "legislation" is any process of making law. According to this definition, the creation and evolution of the common law by the courts is correctly referred to as "judicial legislation." Examples of where the common law has played a dominant role include the law of torts (e.g., negligence, slander), property (e.g., title to land) noncommercial contracts, etc.

In the main, common law develops on a case-by-case basis as the court confronts particular facts before it. No court will announce in the abstract that it has decided to create a new tort or that it is going to abolish a certain defense to a common law action. It is only when a specific controversy has arisen and has been brought to the court by litigants that it will make such pronouncements. Even in these cases, the court rarely is this dramatic in its creation of common law. The vast majority of such law comes into existence through narrow additions to and subtractions from general principles as the court responds to specific facts in the litigation before it. Indeed, if it goes beyond these specific facts in its statement of legal principles, the court is providing what is called *dictum* which is anything the court says that is not necessary to resolve the dispute arising out of the actual facts currently before it.

By definition, statutory law is superior in authority to common law. The legislature has the power to pass statutes that change the common law. When it does so, it has given us what is called a statute *in derogation of the common law.*

2. ENACTED LAW

Enacted law is law created by a governmental body other than a court:

Enacted Law	*Adopted or Created By*
Statute	Legislature
Ordinance	City Council
Regulation	Administrative Agency
Constitution	Constitutional Convention and a combination of action by the legislature and the voters

Enacted law is initiated mainly to govern and to regulate *categories* of persons, events, or things. Most enacted law is written to solve broad problems in society, e.g., pollution control, revenue collection, traffic congestion, crime detection. This is quite different from the process of creating common law by the courts. Common law develops out of concrete controversies involving *specific* individuals, events, and things. Unlike the legislature in the enactment of statutory law, for example, the courts do not initiate and devise common law in order to respond to broad categories of people, events and things. Courts resolve specific disputes, and in the process, they create common law.[1]

The primary focus of this book is on statutes, although the methodology of legislative analysis which we will explore is also relevant to other kinds of enacted law. Furthermore, as we study statutes, we also will view them in the context of regulations and constitutions.

The separation-of-powers doctrine is the starting point in understanding the court's role in applying statutes. Most constitutions place the legislative power within the legislature. For example:

> "All legislative Powers herein granted shall be vested in a Congress . . . ." U.S. Const. art. I, § 1.

> "The Legislative authority of this State shall be vested in a General Assembly . . . ." Tenn. Const. art. 2, § 3.

It would clearly violate the Constitution for a court to create or amend a statute. This would be a usurpation of the legislative power.

A distinction must be made between the *wisdom* of a statute and its *meaning.* In the process of interpreting a statute, a court must not second-guess the wisdom of the legislature in

---

1. Some courts have the power to promulgate procedural rules that govern the technicalities of litigation and the practice of law, e.g., the format that must be used in filing a brief, the steps an attorney must go through to become a member of the bar. In this limited area, the court is regulating categories of events and people rather than resolving specific controversies. Hence these rules also could be classified as enacted law.

passing it. Suppose, for example, that the court is interpreting the following statute:

> § 61. All children of deceased employees shall be entitled to
> receive maintenance benefits from the state.

Assume that the question before the court is whether § 61
requires children of deceased employees to prove that they
were *dependent* on the deceased before death in order to receive the benefits. An adult child who moved out of the
deceased's home years ago is now claiming benefits under
the statute. The agency administering the statute denies the
benefits since this person has not established that he or she
was dependent on the deceased immediately before death.
The person challenges this action in court on the ground that
§ 61 does not require dependency. One of the arguments of
the agency is that the funds from which benefits are paid
would soon be depleted if *any* child can receive benefits
whether or not that child was dependent on the deceased.

There are two ways to view the agency's argument, only
the second of which can be given a receptive ear by the
court:

• It would be ridiculous to allow nondependent children to
receive maintenance benefits under § 61 since this would
soon deplete all of the public resources available.
• To allow nondependent children to receive benefits would
soon deplete all public resources available; the legislature
could not have intended this result; when it wrote § 61, it
meant to cover only dependent children.

The first position amounts to an argument that a statute
covering nondependent children would be a very unwise and
inappropriate statute. The court must reject this argument.
A party making this argument must be told to address it to
the legislature: go to the legislature and try to have the statute changed; it is not the function of a court to determine
whether a statute represents sound public policy. Courts
cannot change statutes.

The second argument (which we shall explore later under
the topic of the golden rule, p. 81) *is* an appropriate argument

before a court. The argument is sensitive to the delicate relationship between courts and legislatures. The court is not being asked to change a statute because it is unwise. The court is being asked to examine the arguably inappropriate consequence of interpreting the statute in a certain way and to determine whether the legislature could have intended such a consequence. If not, then the court may decide to reject this interpretation of the statute on the ground that the *legislature* did not intend it. Here the court would not be usurping the legislative power by changing a statute; it would be carrying out the legislature's will according to the court's perception of legislative intent.

Keeping in mind the distinction between the wisdom of a statute and its meaning, the following is a list of traditional functions that courts properly perform in connection with statutes:

• Interpret the meaning of an individual statute.

• Interpret the meaning of several statutes in relationship to each other, e.g., is one statute inconsistent with another, did the legislature impliedly repeal the earlier statute?

• Interpret the meaning of a statute in relationship to a constitutional provision, e.g., is the statute invalid because it violates the constitution?

• Interpret the meaning of a statute in relationship to a common law doctrine, e.g., did the statute change the common law?

• Interpret the meaning of the statute in relationship to a regulation of an agency, e.g., is the regulation validily based on the statute?

In each instance the process of analysis is rooted in the court's perception of legislative intent.

The discussion thus far on the court's relationship to the legislature may give you the impression that the court's role is primarily mechanical: it is the servant of the legislature; its function is simply to "find" the meaning intended by the legislature and to apply this meaning without trespassing into the realm of wisdom or policy. (This is quite different from its role in a common law case, where the court *does* have the power to create law based on its own conception of wisdom and policy.)

In theory, the court's role in applying statutes is very limited because of the doctrine of separation of powers. In practice, however, the court often has a major *creative* role in the application of statutes. This is due to the nature (a) of language and (b) of the legislative process.

In 1717, Bishop Hoadly spoke of the enormous power of an interpreter:

> Whoever hath an *absolute authority* to *interpret* any written or spoken laws, it is *he* who is truly the law-giver to all intents and purposes, and not the person who first wrote or spoke them. J. Gray, *The Nature and Sources of the Law,* 125 (2d ed. 1921)

Although overstated, there is considerable truth in this observation. As courts interpret a statute, they give it shape and help build it into something that was not there prior to the interpretation. The process of interpreting a law inevitably brings about the ongoing *formulation* of that law.

The clearest example of this is when the legislature uses vague or general language in its statute. The language, in effect, amounts to an invitation to the courts to create law, with this language as the starting point. For example, consider the role of the judiciary in a state with the following statute:

> § 25(b). Divorce shall be granted in this state upon a showing of cruelty.

That's it. No further statutes on cruelty exist. No definition of cruelty is provided by the legislature. Section 25(b) is hardly self-executing! Courts in this state have a very large *creative* role in giving shape to this statute as they try to define cruelty:

• Is it gross indignities according to a reasonable person?

• Is it gross indignities according to the subjective views of one of the spouses?

- Is it conduct which leads to physical impairment of the body? Can conduct causing "only" mental distress be enough?
- Is cruelty the same as incompatibility?
- Is the standard for cruelty different depending upon the length of the marriage and whether children exist?
- Does cruelty exist only if one of the spouses is innocent?
- Etc.

These are questions that the legislature has "dumped" onto the courts. Other examples are statutes that declare contracts, combinations, or trusts "in restraint of trade" to be illegal; or that provide worker's compensation for injuries that "arise out of and in the course of employment." When is a contract "in restraint of trade"? When does an injury "arise out of" employment? The legislature, in effect, has asked the courts to figure out answers to such questions. This is hardly a mechanical responsibility. According to Justice Harlan, when judges are applying broad statutory language, "we may assume that we are free to adopt and shape policies limited only by the most general statement of purpose" from the legislature. Welsh v. United States, 398 U.S. 333, 346, 90 S.Ct. 1792, 1800, 26 L.Ed.2d 308 (1970) (concurring opinion). The broader the language used in a law, the greater will be the court's creative role in interpreting the law and in helping to develop the policy behind it.

Assignment # 3

Assume that the president of your university walks into your class and announces that a mob of students has just taken over several buildings on campus. The president asks for your help. You are given authority "to restore order and to protect life and property at this institution."

a. Make a list of some of the things that you are permitted to do under this authorization.

b. Make a list of some of the things that you think you are not permitted to do under this authorization.

c. In class, read aloud one of the more drastic steps that you listed in "a" above. The rest of the class will act as a court in determining whether you went too far. Be prepared to give dissenting opinions if you disagree with your colleagues on the court.

Perhaps you think that broad and general language in a statute gives too much power to the judiciary. At times, legislatures take this position, and hence try to be more specific in the language that they use in statutes. Do you think that this approach makes Bishop Hoadly's observation less accurate? The Internal Revenue Code suggests otherwise. Taxation statutes tend to be extraordinarily specific and detailed. For example:

> § 404(a)(3)(A). In addition, any amount paid into the trust in any taxable year in excess of the amount allowable with respect to such year under the preceding provisions of this subparagraph shall be deductible in the succeeding years in order of time, but the amount so deductible under this sentence in any one such succeeding taxable year together with the amount allowable under the first sentence of this subparagraph shall not exceed 15 percent of the compensation otherwise paid or accrued during such taxable year to the beneficiaries under the plan.

The moment such a statute is passed, hordes of tax lawyers and accountants comb through it looking for holes and possible ambiguities. They are quite ingenious in developing interpretations that try to walk through these holes and take advantage of the ambiguities. Consequently, fact situations arise which the legislature could not possibly have anticipated. These facts inevitably raise questions about the meaning of the statute: what is a "trust," when is an amount paid "in excess," what is meant by "in order of time," etc.? Nor is this phenomenon limited to tax legislation. No legislator or drafter of legislation can foresee every fact situation that could arise under a given statute no matter how carefully written or how long it is.

In short, whether statutory language is broad or precise, the courts can rarely, if every, be reduced to a mechanical role. The nature of language itself as a vehicle of communication will not allow it. The giants of the law have consistently reminded us of this reality:

Justice Holmes
> A word is not a crystal, transparent and unchanged, it is the skin of a living thought and may vary greatly in color and context according to the circumstances and the time in which it is used. Towne v. Eisner, 245 U.S. 418, 425, 38 S.Ct. 158, 159, 62 L.Ed. 372 (1918).

Judge Hand
> [W]hen you are interpreting words, you must remember that they cover many diverse instances, which cannot be foreseen. Interpretation is necessarily an art of creative imagination; you must try to put yourself in the place of the author of those words and fabricate how he would have dealt with the instance that has arisen. . . . The duty of ascertaining [an enacted law's] meaning is difficult enough at best, and one certain way of missing it is by reading it literally, for words are such temperamental beings that the surest way to lose their essence is to take them at their face value. Judge Learned Hand, *Remarks on Completion of Fifty Years of Federal Judicial Service* (Robert LeFlar, Appellate Judicial Opinions 72–3 (1974); in addition see 264 F.2d 1, 27 (1959).

Judge Traynor
> An insistence upon judicial regard for the words of a statute does not imply that they are like words in a dictionary, to be read with no ranging of the mind. They are no longer at rest in their alphabetical bins. Released, combined in phrases that imperfectly communicate the thoughts of one man to another, they challenge men to give them more than passive reading, to consider well their context, to ponder what may be their consequences. People v. Knowles, 35 Cal.2d 175, 182, 217 P.2d 1, 5 (1950).

Further complicating the picture is the nature of the legislative process itself. Most legislatures consist of hundreds of elected officials who operate in a highly political environment. Legislators often bargain for each other's votes. ("I'll vote in favor of your bill on firearms if you will support the bill to fund the water project in my district.") It is not uncommon for legislation to be passed in a crisis atmosphere where few legislators have the time, interest, or expertise to read and understand everything that they are voting for. Hence, there is no such thing as a collective legislative mind which has a readily identifiable intent accompanying every statute that is passed.

It is not surprising, therefore, that courts are frequently charged with usurping the legislative role by rewriting a statute under the guise of interpreting it. Courts operate under substantial handicaps that almost make this charge inevitable:

- Statutes are often written in broad and vague language.
- All language is inherently weak as a vehicle of communication.
- Legislatures could not possibly anticipate every fact situation that could arise under a statute.
- Legislative intent can be extremely difficult to identify due to the fractional nature of the legislative process.

While the separation-of-powers doctrine remains the guiding principle in this area, the above realities suggest that the line that separates the legislative from the judicial branches of government can be a thin and fragile line.

FRANKFURTER, F., "SOME REFLECTIONS ON THE READING OF STATUTES" [1]

Difficulties of Construction

. . . Anything that is written may present a problem of meaning, and that is the essence of the business of judges

---

1. Copyright © 1983 by the director of the Columbia Law Review Association, Inc. All rights reserved. This article originally appeared at 47 Colum.L.Rev. 527–546 (1947). Reprinted by permission.

in construing legislation.   The problem derives from the very nature of words.   They are symbols of meaning.   But unlike mathematical symbols, the phrasing of a document, especially a complicated enactment, seldom attains more than approximate precision.   If individual words are inexact symbols, with shifting variables, their configuration can hardly achieve invariant meaning or assured definiteness.   Apart from the ambiguity inherent in its symbols, a statute suffers from dubieties.   It is not an equation or a formula representing a clearly marked process, nor is it an expression of individual thought to which is imparted the definiteness a single authorship can give.   A statute is an instrument of government partaking of its practical purposes but also of its infirmities and limitations, of its awkward and groping efforts.   With one of his flashes of insight, Mr. Justice Johnson called the science of government "the science of experiment."[2]   The phrase, uttered a hundred and twenty-five years ago, has a very modern ring, for time has only served to emphasize its accuracy.   To be sure, laws can measurably be improved with improvement in the mechanics of legislation, and the need for interpretation is usually in inverse ratio to the care and imagination of draftsmen.   .   .   .

The difficulties are inherent not only in the nature of words, of composition, and of legislation generally.   They are often intensified by the subject matter of an enactment.   The imagination which can draw an income tax statute to cover the myriad transactions of a society like ours, capable of producing the necessary revenue without producing a flood of litigation, has not yet revealed itself.   Moreover, government sometimes solves problems by shelving them temporarily.   The legislative process reflects that attitude.   Statutes as well as constitutional provisions at times embody purposeful ambiguity or are expressed with a generality for future unfolding.   .   .   .

The intrinsic difficulties of language and the emergence after enactment of situations not anticipated by the most gifted legislative imagination, reveal doubts and ambiguities

---

2. Anderson v. Dunn, 19 U.S. (6 Wheat.) 204, 226 (1821).

in statutes that compel judicial construction. The process of construction, therefore, is not an exercise in logic or dialectic: the aids of formal reasoning are not irrelevant; they may simply be inadequate. The purpose of construction being the ascertainment of meaning, every consideration brought to bear for the solution of that problem must be devoted to that end alone. To speak of it as a practical problem is not to indulge a fashion in words. It must be that, not something else. Not, for instance, an opportunity for a judge to use words as "empty vessels into which he can pour anything he will"—his caprices, fixed notions, even statesmanlike beliefs in a particular policy. Nor, on the other hand, is the process a ritual to be observed by unimaginative adherence to well-worn professional phrases. To be sure, it is inescapably a problem in the keeping of the legal profession and subject to all the limitations of our adversary system of adjudication. When the judge, selected by society to give meaning to what the legislature has done, examines the statute, he does so not in a laboratory or in a classroom. Damage has been done or exactions made, interests are divided, passions have been aroused, sides have been taken. But the judge, if he is worth his salt, must be above the battle. We must assume in him not only personal impartiality but intellectual disinterestedness. In matters of statutory construction also it makes a great deal of difference whether you start with an answer or with a problem.

    . . . [L]aws are not abstract propositions. They are expressions of policy arising out of specific situations and addressed to the attainment of particular ends. The difficulty is that the legislative ideas which laws embody are both explicit and immanent. And so the bottom problem is: What is below the surface of the words and yet fairly a part of them? Words in statutes are not unlike words in a foreign language in that they too have "associations, echoes, and overtones." [3] Judges must retain the associations, hear the echoes, and capture the overtones. In one of his very last opinions, dealing with legislation taxing the husband on

---

3. Barker, The Politics of Aristotle lxiii (1946).

the basis of the combined income of husband and wife, Holmes wrote: "The statutes are the outcome of a thousand years of history. . . . They form a system with echoes of different moments, none of which is entitled to prevail over the other." [4]

What exactions such a duty of construction places upon judges, and with what freedom it entrusts them! John Chipman Gray was fond of quoting from a sermon by Bishop Hoadly that "Whoever hath an *absolute authority* to *interpret* any written or spoken laws, it is he who is truly the law-giver to all intents and purposes, and not the person who first wrote or spoke them." [5] By admitting that there is some substance to the good Bishop's statement, one does not subscribe to the notion that they are law-givers in any but a very qualified sense.

Even within their area of choice the courts are not at large. They are confined by the nature and scope of the judicial function in its particular exercise in the field of interpretation. They are under the constraints imposed by the judicial function in our democratic society. As a matter of verbal recognition certainly, no one will gainsay that the function in construing a statute is to ascertain the meaning of words used by the legislature. To go beyond it is to usurp a power which our democracy has lodged in its elected legislature. The great judges have constantly admonished their brethren of the need for discipline in observing the limitations. A judge must not rewrite a statute, neither to enlarge nor to contract it. Whatever temptations the statesmanship of policy-making might wisely suggest, construction must eschew interpolation and evisceration. He must not read in by way of creation. He must not read out except to avoid patent nonsense or internal contradiction. "If there is no meaning in it," said Alice [in Wonderland's] King, "that saves a world of trouble, you know, as we needn't try to find any." Legislative words presumably have meaning and so we must try to find it.

---

4. Hoeper v. Tax Commission, 284 U.S. 206, 219 (1931).

5. Gray, Nature and Sources of the Law, 102, 125, 172 (2d ed. 1921).

This duty of restraint, this humility of function as merely the translator of another's command, is a constant theme of our Justices. It is on the lips of all judges, but seldom, I venture to believe, has the restraint which it expresses, or the duty which it enjoins, been observed with so consistent a realization that its observance depends on self-conscious discipline. Cardozo put it this way: "We do not pause to consider whether a statute differently conceived and framed would yield results more consonant with fairness and reason. We take this statute as we find it." [6] It was expressed more fully by Mr. Justice Brandeis when the temptation to give what might be called a more liberal interpretation could not have been wanting. "The particularization and detail with which the scope of each provision, the amount of the tax thereby imposed, and the incidence of the tax, were specified, preclude an extension of any provision by implication to any other subject. . . . What the [party] . . . asks is not a construction of a statute, but, in effect, an enlargement of it by the court, so that what was omitted, presumably by inadvertence, may be included within its scope." [7] An omission at the time of enactment, whether careless or calculated, cannot be judicially supplied however much later wisdom may recommend the inclusion.

Legislation has an aim; it seeks to obviate some mischief, to supply an inadequacy, to effect a change of policy, to formulate a plan of government. That aim, that policy is not drawn, like nitrogen, out of the air; it is evinced in the language of the statute, as read in the light of other external manifestations of purpose. That is what the judge must seek and effecuate, . . .

Violence must not be done to the words chosen by the legislature. Unless indeed no doubt can be left that the legislature has in fact used a private code, so that what appears to be violence to language is merely respect to special usage. In the end, language and external aids, each accorded the authority deserved in the circumstances, must be weighed in

---

6. Anderson v. Wilson, 289 U.S. 20, 27 (1933).
7. Iselin v. United States, 270 U.S. 245, 250, 251 (1926).

the balance of judicial judgment. Only if its premises are emptied of their human variables, can the process of statutory construction have the precision of a syllogism. We cannot avoid what Mr. Justice Cardozo deemed inherent in the problem of construction, making "a choice between uncertainties. We must be content to choose the lesser."[8]

The quality of legislative organization and procedure is inevitably reflected in the quality of legislative draftsmanship. Representative Monroney told the House last July that "ninety-five percent of all the legislation that becomes law passes the Congress in the shape that it came from our committees. Therefore if our committee work is sloppy, if it is bad, if it is inadequate, our legislation in ninety-five percent of the cases will be bad and inadequate as well."[9] And Representative Lane added that ". . . in the second session of the 78th Congress 953 bills and resolutions were passed, of which only 86 were subject to any real discussion."[10] But what courts do with legislation may in turn deeply affect what Congress will do in the future. Emerson says somewhere that mankind is as lazy as it dares to be. Loose judicial reading makes for loose legislative writing. It encourages the practice illustrated in a recent cartoon in which a senator tells his colleagues "I admit this new bill is too complicated to understand. We'll just have to pass it to find out what it means." A modern Pascal might be tempted at times to say of legislation what Pascal said of students of theology when he charged them with "a looseness of thought and language that would pass nowhere else in making what are professedly very fine distinctions." And it is conceivable that he might go on and speak, as did Pascal, of the "insincerity with which terms are carefully chosen to cover opposite meanings."[11]

But there are more fundamental objections to loose judicial reading. In a democracy the legislative impulse and its expression should come from those popularly chosen to leg-

---

8. Burnet v. Guggenheim, 288 U.S. 280, 288 (1933).

9. 92 Cong. Rec. 10040 (1946).

10. 92 Cong. Rec. 10054 (1946).

11. Pater, *Essay on Pascal* in Miscellaneous Studies 48, 51 (1895).

islate, and equipped to devise policy, as courts are not. The pressure on legislatures to discharge their responsibility with care, understanding and imagination should be stiffened, not relaxed. Above all, they must not be encouraged in irresponsible or undisciplined use of language. In the keeping of legislatures perhaps more than any other group is the well-being of their fellow-men. Their responsibility is discharged ultimately by words. They are under a special duty therefore to observe that "Exactness in the use of words is the basis of all serious thinking. You will get nowhere without it. Words are clumsy tools, and it is very easy to cut one's fingers with them, and they need the closest attention in handling; but they are the only tools we have, and imagination itself cannot work without them. You must master the use of them, or you will wander forever guessing at the mercy of mere impulse and unrecognized assumptions and arbitrary associations, carried away with every wind of doctrine." [12]

Perfection of draftsmanship is as unattainable as demonstrable correctness of judicial reading of legislation. Fit legislation and fair adjudication are attainable. The ultimate reliance of society for the proper fulfilment of both these august functions is to entrust them only to those who are equal to their demands.

Assignment # 4

a. Why would a legislature engage in "purposeful ambiguity" in a statute?

b. To what extent is it undemocratic for the courts to help shape (rather than merely identify) policy through the interpretation of broad statutory language?

c. How would you sum up Justice Frankfurter's views on the role of the courts in interpreting statutes? Assume that you are giving a brief presentation to a group of new judges on their role. Using Justice Frankfurter as your mentor, what would you say?

---

12. Allen, *Essay on Jeremy Bentham* in The Social and Political Ideas of the Revolutionary Era 181, 199 (Hearnshaw ed. 1931).

Chapter 2

Preliminary Problems
of Interpretation

This chapter presents some preliminary problems of interpretation. While there is a drafting component to each of the problems, the focus is not on the mechanics of drafting. These mechanics are covered later. The theme of the problems is analysis, but from a variety of perspectives. In Chapter One we learned from Holmes, Hand, Traynor, and Frankfurter that language is a very vulnerable tool. The problems that follow are designed to explore this conclusion in concrete situations before we begin our study of principles or rules of interpretation and drafting. In an introductory way, the goal is to increase our understanding of the process of interpretation by examining the spectrum of legislation from the different but interrelated perspectives of the drafter, the advocate, and the judge. One of the best ways to appreciate the complexities and skills involved in any one of these perspectives is to assume the role of all three.

Instructions for Assignments # # 5–8

a. You are a member of the state legislature with the responsibility of drafting a statute with the objective indicated in the assignment. Draft the statute *without* looking at the facts in the problems to which your statute will be later applied. Also, there is no need to consult Chapter Fourteen on the mechanics of writing legislation. Draft your statute from the vantage point of someone new to the field. Draw on the writing and problem-solving skills that you have brought with you to the course.

b. After you draft the statute, turn to the problems for your statute. Determine whether your statute applies to the facts in the problems. Be sure to give arguments for and against the applicability of your statute where differing viewpoints are reasonable. You have the full reign of an advocate in arguing your interpretations, but you cannot change the statute.

c. After you have applied the statute for those problems that go with the statute, redraft the statute if you think that redrafting is necessary after having gone through step "b" above.

Assignment # 5

(The problems that go with this assignment are problems A and B below, but the drafter should not read these problems before drafting.)

You are a member of the state legislature. There have been many reports of drownings in your state where there were spectators who did not come to the rescue of the person who drowned. Draft a statute making it a misdemeanor for anyone to fail to aid someone who is drowning. Your statute will become § 22 of the State Penal Code.

Assignment # 6

(The problems that go with this assignment are problems C and D below, but the drafter should not read these problems before drafting.)

Assignment # 6—Continued

You are a member of the state legislature. The present state income tax law requires every citizen of the state to file an income tax return regardless of whether he or she has any tax to pay. You feel that it is an unnecessary burden to ask people who do not have any tax to pay to file a tax return. You think that senior citizens, for example, who live exclusively on nontaxable income should not have to file a state income tax return. Draft a statute which waives the requirement of filing a tax return for those who have no taxes to pay. Your statute will be § 55.7 of the State Internal Revenue Code.

Assignment # 7

(The problems that go with this assignment are problems E and F below, but the drafter should not read these problems before drafting.)

You are a member of the state legislature. Many people die with wills that say, "I leave my property to my heirs." There has been some confusion in the state as to whether "heirs" includes adopted children of the deceased or only blood children. You decide to draft a statute which will specify that the word "heirs" shall include adopted children. Your statute will be § 209 of the State Probate Code.

Assignment # 8

(The problems that go with this assignment are problems G and H below, but the drafter should not read these problems before drafting.)

You are a member of the state legislature. There are no statutes in your state which would allow parents to institutionalize minors who cannot be controlled or disciplined by their parents. Draft a statute which would give the Family Court this power. Your statute will become § 649 of the Family Code.

Problem A

Apply § 22 (from Assignment # 5) to the following facts:

The state prosecutor is charging Jones and Smith with violating § 22. Smith was in his own back yard. His neighbor, Jones, had her eight-month-old baby sitting in a portable pool (three feet in diameter, one-half foot deep). There was about four inches of water in the pool. Smith and Jones had never been friendly neighbors. Jones had put up a four-foot fence in her yard expressly to keep Smith and his family out. Jones went in the house for a moment. Suddenly the baby fell from a sitting position to a lying down position in the pool. Smith calls over to Jones in her house about the danger. Jones tells Smith to mind his own business. Smith does nothing more. The baby drowns. Does § 22 apply?

Problem B

Apply § 22 (from Assignment # 5) to the following facts:

The state prosecutor is charging Peters with violating § 22. Peters and his son were in a canoe on the river. Thompson and his son were also on the same river in another canoe. Peters sees Thompson fall out of the canoe. Peters is scared. He must make a choice: go after Thompson by paddling toward him, or take his own canoe to the shore where he and his son can be safe. He decides to go to the shore. Thompson drowns. Does § 22 apply?

Problem C

Apply § 55.7 (from Assignment # 6) to the following facts:

The state tax commissioner claims that Richardson has illegally failed to file an income tax return. Richardson lives on non-taxable government benefits. During the year, however, he performed one odd job for about an hour. The income he got from this job was so small that if he had filed his return he would have owed the state 38 cents in taxes. He did not file a tax return. Does § 55.7 apply?

Problem D

Apply § 55.7 (from Assignment # 6) to the following facts:

The state tax commissioner claims that Stevenson has illegally failed to file an income tax return. Stevenson had over

$150,000 in income during the year but would have had to pay no state taxes because he had more than enough legitimate state deductions to offset all of his income. Hence, he did not file a tax return. Does § 55.7 apply?

Problem E

Apply § 209 (from Assignment # 7) to the following facts:

While Stephonson is married to Alice, he adopts Brown. When Brown is 17 years old, he runs away from home and is never heard from until the day Stephonson dies, 37 years later. Four years after Brown disappeared, Stephonson and Alice obtained a divorce. Stephonson then married Martha. One son is born to them: Sam. When Stephonson dies, his will says that he leaves all his property to "my heirs." Brown claims that he is entitled to receive property under the will. Sam contests this claim; he feels that he should receive all the property. Does § 209 apply?

Problem F

Apply § 209 (from Assignment # 7) to the following facts:

Sullivan is the adopted son of Carter. Sullivan knows that Carter has a will leaving his estate "to my heirs." Sullivan murders Carter in order to collect under the will. Sullivan is tried and convicted of murder. While in prison, Sullivan makes a claim for his share of the estate. This claim is contested by Carter's only living kin, his (blood) son, Frank. Does § 209 apply?

Problem G

Apply § 649 (from Assignment # 8) to the following facts:

Bob is 10 years old. His mother and father are dead. He has been taken care of by his 24-year-old sister, Brenda. Brenda is out of work for a long time so that she can be home to care for Bob. She now obtains a full-time job. There are no other relatives, and Brenda no longer wants the responsibility for Bob. She wants to institutionalize him. Does § 649 apply?

Problem H

Apply § 649 (from Assignment # 8) to the following facts:

Cathy is 13 years old. Her father is dead. Her mother is frequently drunk. Cathy and her mother argue a lot. Cathy is a very good student in school and has a good relationship with everyone in the neighborhood. She has no other relatives. Her mother wants the state to take care of Cathy since she feels that Cathy is a problem too big for her to handle. Does § 649 apply?

Assignment # 9

The building at 137 Dock Street is owned by the state government. The building is open from 6 AM to midnight every day, but the main hours of work for the vast majority of employees is 8:30 AM to 6 PM. One of the rooms on the third floor (Room 326) is used only occasionally by the staff. The director of the agency that occupies the building wants to make Room 326 available to the community and asks the staff to draft a rule that would make this possible in an orderly manner.

Every student in the classroom will be divided into one of two groups: Group 1 and Group 2. The two groups meet in separate corners of the classroom.

Instructions for Group 1

Appoint one student as the reporter who will take notes on what is agreed upon. After a brief discussion, draft the rule on Room 326. Assume that the director is out of town for three months and will not be available to you.

Instructions for Group 2

Appoint one student as the reporter who will take notes. Invent 10 to 15 fact situations involving individual(s) in the community who might want to use Room 326. State the circumstances of each situation: who wants to use the room, why, when, etc. Try to think of situations that might pose difficulties of various kinds on the use of the room.

The two groups then convene in the classroom. The reporter for Group 1 writes the rule on the blackboard or on a flip chart. The reporter for Group 2 reads individual fact situations prepared by this group. The class then discusses whether the rule applies to each of the situations. What are the arguments that the rule permits use of Room 326 in the fact situation under discussion? What are the arguments that the rule would not permit use? Pay particular attention to words or phrases in the rule that need to be defined. Which definitions support use? Which support nonuse?

At the end of the discussion, each student (regardless of which group he or she was initially in) must redraft the rule. The student works alone in preparing this draft.

Instructions for Assignments # # 10 to 12

a. In each assignment there is an interpretation of a statute or regulation as applied to a given set of facts. Prepare arguments for and against the validity of this interpretation.

b. For each assignment, two students will be selected to give oral presentations on the validity of the interpretation, one for and one against. They will debate their respective views with each other in the classroom.

c. After the debate, the class will discuss how the statute or regulation could be redrafted to eliminate any ambiguity that may have been identified during the debate.

d. Each student will then individually redraft the statute or regulation and prepare a written analysis on how the new draft would apply to the original set of facts.

Assignment # 10

Statute: § 15.4(b). Name of Corporation

The articles of incorporation shall contain:

The name of the proposed corporation, which shall include the word "company", "corporation", "incorporated", or such other word, abbreviation, affix, or prefix as will clearly indicate that it is a corporation instead of a natural person or partnership. The name shall be such as will distinguish it from any other corporation authorized to do business in Florida.

Facts: A new catsup company has been organized in Florida. It wants to call itself the Pepsi Catsup Company. The Pepsi Cola Bottling Company (which is authorized to do business in Florida) claims that this name would violate § 15.4(b).

Interpretation: The name "Pepsi Catsup Company" is an allowable corporate name in Florida because one can "distinguish" it from the name of the Pepsi Cola Bottling Company pursuant to § 15.4(b).

Assignment # 11

Statute: § 19.   Powers of Probation Officer

A probation officer does not have the powers of a law enforcement officer. A probation officer may take into custody and place in detention a child who is under his supervision as a delinquent child or as a child in need of supervision when the probation officer has reasonable cause to believe that the child has violated the conditions of his probation.

Facts: Casey is a Probation Officer who is supervising Linda, a delinquent child on probation. One of the conditions of Linda's probation is that she not leave the city. One day Casey gets an anonymous phone call that Linda is five miles outside the city limits. Casey goes to check this out and finds Linda outside the city. He therefore takes her into custody pursuant to § 19. Linda admits that she left the city, but argues that § 19 was violated because Casey had no "reasonable cause to believe" that she had violated a condition of her probation.

Interpretation: Casey had "reasonable cause to believe" Linda violated a condition of her probation.

Assignment # 12

Regulation: § 1.119–1.   Meals and lodgings furnished for the convenience of the employer.

(a) Meals. The value of meals furnished to an employee by his employer shall be excluded from the employee's gross income if two tests are met: (i) The meals are furnished on the business premises of the employer, and (ii) the meals are furnished for the convenience of the employer. The question of whether meals are furnished for the convenience of the employer is one of fact to be determined by analysis of all the facts and circumstances in each case.

(b) Lodging. The value of lodging furnished to an employee by the employer shall be excluded from the employee's gross income if three tests are met:

(1) The lodging is furnished on the business premises of the employer,

(2) The lodging is furnished for the convenience of the employer, and

(3) The employee is required to accept such lodging as a condition of his employment.

The requirement of subparagraph (3) of this paragraph that the employee is required to accept such lodging as a condition of his employment means that he be required to accept the lodging in order to enable him properly to perform the duties of his employment. Lodging will be regarded as furnished to enable the employee properly to perform the duties of his employment when, for example, the lodging is furnished because the employee is required to be available for duty at all times or because the employee could not perform the services required of him unless he is furnished such lodging.

Facts: Pat is a member of the Peace Corps in Algeria. She receives $100 a month as living expenses. The Peace Corps office in Washington, D.C., sends her this check each month after deducting federal income taxes. Pat claims (and can substantiate) that $85 of this $100 each month goes for the payment of her rent and food bills. She wants to deduct this $85 from her gross income under § 1.119–1(a) and (b).

Interpretation: The $85 deduction is not allowable because the tests in § 1.119–1(a)(i) and (ii) have not been met, and the tests in § 1.119–1(b)(1)(2) and (3) have not been met.

REGINA v. OJIBWAY

8 Criminal Law Quarterly 137
(Toronto 1965)

BLUE, J. This is an appeal by the Crown by way of a stated case from a decision of the magistrate acquitting the accused of a charge under the Small Birds Act, R.S.O., 1960, c. 724, § 2. The facts are not in dispute. Fred Ojibway, an Indian, was riding his pony through Queen's Park on January 2, 1965. Being impoverished, and having been forced to pledge his saddle, he substituted a downy pillow in lieu of the said saddle. On this particular day the accused's misfortune was further heightened by the circumstance of his pony breaking its right foreleg. In accord with Indian custom, the accused then shot the pony to relieve it of its awkwardness.

The accused was then charged with having breached the Small Birds Act, § 2, of which states:

> 2. Anyone maiming, injuring, or killing small birds is guilty of an offence and subject to a fine not in excess of two hundred dollars.

The learned magistrate acquitted the accused holding, in fact, that he had killed his horse and not a small bird. With respect, I cannot agree.

In light of the definition section my course is quite clear. Section 1 defines "bird" as "a two legged animal covered with feathers." There can be no doubt that this case is covered by this section.

Counsel for the accused made several ingenious arguments to which, in fairness, I must address myself. He submitted that the evidence of the expert clearly concluded that the animal in question was a pony and not a bird, but this is not the issue. We are not interested in whether the animal in question is a bird or not in fact, but whether it is one in law. Statutory interpretation has forced many a horse to eat birdseed for the rest of its life.

Counsel also contended that the neighing noise emitted by the animal could not possibly be produced by a bird. With respect, the sounds emitted by an animal are irrelevant to its nature, for a bird is no less a bird because it is silent.

Counsel for the accused also argues that since there was evidence to show accused had ridden the animal, this pointed to the fact that it could not be a bird but was actually a pony. Obviously, this avoids the issue. The issue is not whether the animal was ridden or not, but whether it was shot or not, for to ride a pony or a bird is of no offence at all. I believe counsel now sees his mistake.

Counsel contends that the iron shoes found on the animal decisively disqualify it from being a bird. I must inform counsel, however, that how an animal dresses is of no concern to this court.

Counsel relied on the decision in Re Chicadee, where he contends that in similar circumstances the accused was acquitted. However, this is a horse of a different colour. A close reading of that case indicates that the animal in question there was not a small bird but, in fact, a midget of a much larger species. Therefore, that case is inapplicable to our facts.

Counsel finally submits that the word "small" in the title Small Birds Act refers not to "Birds" but to "Act", making it The Small Act relating to Birds. With respect, counsel did not do his homework very well, for the Large Birds Act, R.S.O.1960, c. 725, is just as small. If pressed, I need only refer to the Small Loans Act, R.S.O.1960, c. 727, which is twice as large as the Large Birds Act.

It remains then to state my reason for judgment which, simply, is as follows: Different things may take on the same meaning for different purposes. For the purpose of the Small Birds Act, all two-legged, feather-covered animals are birds. This, of course, does not imply that only two-legged animals qualify, for the legislative intent is to make two legs merely the minimum requirement. The statute therefore contemplated multilegged animals with feathers as well. Counsel submits that having regard to the purpose of the statute only small animals "naturally covered" with feathers could have been contemplated. However, had this been the intention of the legislature, I am certain that the phrase "naturally covered" would have been expressly inserted just as "Long" was inserted in the Longshoreman's Act.

Therefore, a horse with feathers on its back must be deemed for the purposes of this act to be a bird and, *a fortiori,* a pony with feathers on its back is a small bird.

Counsel posed the following rhetorical question: If the pillow had been removed prior to the shooting, would the animal still be a bird? To this let me answer rhetorically: Is a bird any less a bird without its feathers?

Appeal allowed.

Reported by: H. Pomerantz
          S. Breslin

Chapter Three

The Legal Environment of a Statute: Methods of Understanding Legislation

Five interrelated questions must be asked whenever you are trying to understand and apply a statute:

a. What is the "plain meaning" of the language in the statute? To what extent is the meaning self-evident?

b. Why was the statute adopted? What needs prompted it? What mischief or evil was the legislature trying to correct?

c. What happened in the legislature during the process of adoption? What is the statute's legislative history?

d. What was the law prior to the adoption of the statute?

e. What has happened since the statute was created? What has been the response of the courts, the agency charged with administering the statute, the legislature, the public, scholars, etc.?

These questions constitute the foundation of the methods of understanding any statute. The answers to the questions will place the statute in context within the legal system. Without this context, any application of the statute is on potentially dangerous ground.

In Figure 1, the various components of the context—or legal environment—of a statute are outlined. Not all of the components will be relevant to every statute, and you will not necessarily pursue them in the order listed here. The components will be briefly examined now, and in greater detail later in the book.

1. THE TEXT OF THE STATUTE AND ITS PLAIN MEANING

The starting point in understanding a statute is the text of the statute itself. Our initial search must be for the "plain meaning" of this text. Usually we rely upon the legislature to say what it means in a statute by its choice of language. Thus we look to the "plain meaning" of the statute. As we have seen, however, language does not always lend itself to clear meanings. The responsibility of being faithful to the text of the statute does not require that we never go beyond the surface of the text. The plain meaning rule, as we shall see in Chapter Five, is but a point of departure and a guideline which cautions us not to go too far in finding meaning that may not be there.

2. PRIOR LAW

A statute in some way changes the law that existed prior to the enactment of the statute. For example, the statute may have changed a prior statute, changed the common law (p. 6), added a totally new area of the law, etc. Perhaps there was a controversial court opinion interpreting an existing statute (or a controversial agency regulation implementing this statute). The legislature may have wanted to make sure that the interpretation of the statute by the courts or by the agency would be different in the future. Consequently, the legislature could have decided to amend the old statute or to create a totally new one. Knowing this prior law can sometimes be helpful in understanding the purpose of the statute

Figure 1. The Legal Environment of a Statute

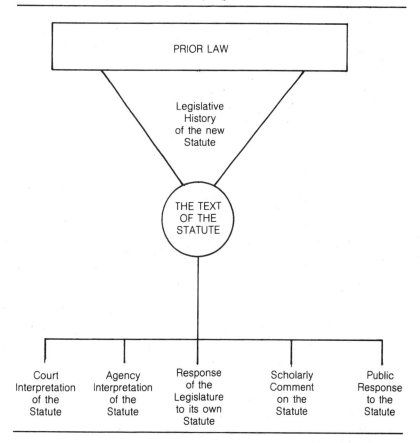

which in turn may provide some guidance in interpreting the language of the statute itself.

There are several places where you can locate the law that existed prior to the passage of a statute. Court opinions interpreting the statute may provide this information (p. 193). It also is usually covered somewhere in the documents of the legislative history of the statute (p. 97). In the code containing the current statute, there is usually a "history" reference which will summarize prior changes in the statute. Finally, if the statute is relatively important, scholars will have commented on it within treatises and legal periodical literature

(p. 194). Such commentary will almost always include a discussion of prior law.

3. LEGISLATIVE HISTORY

Every statute goes through a certain process in the legislature before it becomes a law. Studies and investigations may precede the introduction of the proposed law (i.e., bill) in the legislature. Hearings on the bill may take place in one or both houses of the legislature. Amendments to the bill are common. The committees considering the bill will sometimes prepare reports on the major features of the bill and why it should be passed. There may be debates on the floor of both houses on the merits, meaning, and contemplated impact of the bill. The documents that come out of this process can provide many clues that are helpful in interpreting and applying the statute. As we shall see, however, there are many problems that must be faced before using any of the data of legislative history (p. 103), but the data cannot be ignored.

4. COURT INTERPRETATION OF THE STATUTE

Most statutes that have been "on the books" for some time have been interpreted by the courts. It is obviously very important to find out what the courts have said about the statute. You want to know whether the courts have ever applied the statute to facts that are the same or similar to the facts that are currently in dispute. There are two main ways to find out.

First, you "shepardize" the statute. Go to the set of Shepard's citations covering your statute (e.g., *Shepard's Rhode Island Citations* for a Rhode Island statute or *Shepard's United States Citations* for a federal statute). In the columns of Shepard's, you will find citations or references to any cases that have ever mentioned the statute you are shepardizing. You then take these citations and go to the full text of the cases in a set of books called reporters. (Other useful information provided by Shepard's will be discussed later, p. 197.)

Second, you can find cases that have interpreted the statute by examining the "notes to decisions" that immediately follow the text of the statute in annotated codes. The latter is simply a set of books where all of the statutes are organized by subject matter along with research material on the statute such as notes to decisions. For the most current material, be sure to check the pocket part of the volume that contains your statute and any supplemental pamphlets that are usually found at the end of the code. The notes will consist of small-paragraph summaries of cases. The citations to the cases will also be provided so that you can find their full text in the reporters.

Other techniques of locating opinions interpreting statutes are outlined on p. 193.

5. AGENCY INTERPRETATION OF THE STATUTE

Often an administrative agency is given responsibility by the legislature to carry out a statute, e.g., the State Worker's Compensation Commission or the United States Department of Health and Human Services. To do this, the agency, of course, must interpret the statute. It may issue regulations that specify how the statute will be administered. Also, the agency may have a formal or informal dispute settlement process within the agency to resolve controversies under the statute and regulations. Some agencies publish the results of these proceedings in what are often called agency opinions or administrative decisions. Regulations and administrative decisions, however, can usually be challenged in court where the claim is that the agency, in effect, misinterpreted the statute.

It is sometimes difficult to locate agency regulations and decisions, particularly for state agencies where the system of publication is often haphazard.

For federal agencies, many regulations are published in the *Code of Federal Regulations* and in the *Federal Register.* (There is a table in the index volume of the *Code of Federal Regulations* which will tell you what federal regulations are based on and carry out designated federal statutes.)   Each individual federal agency may or may not publish its own administrative decisions.

A few states have collections of agency regulations roughly comparable to the *Code of Federal Regulations* at the federal level.   Most, however, do not.   You need to contact an area law librarian or the state agency itself to find out what regulations and administrative decisions, if any, are published.

6. RESPONSE OF THE LEGISLATURE TO ITS OWN STATUTE

Once a statute is passed, there may be attempts within the legislature to amend or repeal it.   If the attempts succeed, new statutes will be created which of course must be analyzed.   To determine the current status of a statute, (1) check the pocket part to the volume of the code containing your statute, (2) check supplementary pamphlets at the end of the code, (3) shepardize the statute—Shepard's will list amendments, repeals, etc.), and (4) determine whether there is a "legislative service" which gives information on the activities of the legislature, e.g., Commerce Clearing House's *Congressional Index.*

7. SCHOLARLY COMMENT ON THE STATUTE

Statutes occasionally are difficult to read and understand. One of the methods of obtaining help in interpreting a statute is by checking any scholarly commentary that may have been written on the statute.   In addition, you may be given leads to the legislative history on the statute as well as to cases, regulations, or administrative decisions that you may have overlooked in your research.   Courts sometimes find scholarly commentary on a statute to be persuasive in the adoption of a particular interpretation.

The primary sources of scholarly comment on any legal subject are the legal periodicals, sometimes called law reviews or journals. The three main index systems used to find such material are the *Index to Legal Periodicals, Legal Resource Index,* and *Current Law Index.* Locate the subject headings in these index systems in order to find periodical literature on your statute. To do this, check entries under the topic of your statute. For example, if you are studying a job discrimination statute, examine the subject headings of "employment," "constitutional law," etc. If your statute has a popular name (e.g., the Civil Rights Act of 1964), there also may be statute tables in these index systems which give you references to periodical literature under the popular name of the statute (p. 121).

Treatises are books written by individuals outside the government (or by individuals inside the government writing in a nonofficial capacity) on a given topic. Often these books cover statutory law. Check the card catalog in your law library under the topics in your statute.

8. PUBLIC RESPONSE TO THE STATUTE

Statutes have varying degrees of impact on the community or on society as a whole. Sometimes it is helpful to determine what this impact has been. According to one court:

> A practical construction given a statute by the public generally, as indicated by a uniform course of conduct over a considerable period of time, and acquiesced in and approved by a public official charged with the duty of enforcing the act, is entitled to great weight in the interpretation which should be given it, in case there is any ambiguity in its meaning serious enough to raise a reasonable doubt in any fair mind. Hennessy v. Personal Finance Corp., 176 Misc. 201, 205, 26 N.Y.S.2d 1012, 1017 (Sup.1941).

Has there been widespread compliance or disobedience with the statute? Has the statute caused economic hardships to certain segments of the population? Have there been any great administrative burdens in enforcing the statute?

When seemingly unusual consequences can be identified, you may be able to argue that they have been due to a misinterpretation of the statute by the officials in charge of carrying it out. The argument is that the legislature probably did not intend such consequences. Hence, you are asking the court to adopt an interpretation of the statute that will *avoid* these consequences. (We will examine this argument later under the "golden rule," p. 81.) Of course, if the court determines that these consequences *were* within the intent of the legislature when it passed the statute, you will be told to go to the legislature and try to convince it to change the statute (p. 9).

To locate impact studies on statutes, you may have to check the social science literature in addition to the standard sources of scholarly legal commentary in legal periodicals and treatises. Other sources may be bar association or administrative agency studies on the statute (p. 101).

Chapter Four

Elements, Issues, and Memos

Section A. Codes, Titles, Chapters, Parts, and Sections

The main organizational units of statutes are: code, title, chapter, part, and section. The latter three are often further subdivided into subchapters, subparts, and subsections, respectively. Not all sets of statutes are organized in the same way, although the general format of the sets is often similar.

The word "code" refers to all of the statutes of public interest organized by subject matter rather than chronologically as they are passed, e.g., United States Code, Georgia Code Annotated. In some states the word "Statutes" has the same meaning as code, e.g., Arkansas Statutes Annotated, Colorado Revised Statutes. The word "annotated" simply means that research references are provided along with the full text of the statutes.

While there are differences within various sets of statutes, the pattern of titles, chapters, parts, and sections is often as follows:

- *Subsections* are smaller units within sections
- *Sections* are smaller units within subparts
- *Subparts* are smaller units within parts
- *Parts* are smaller units within subchapters

Figure 2. The Organizational Structure of a Statute

- *Title 8* is within the United States Code

TITLE 8—ALIENS AND NATIONALITY

- *Chapter 12* is within Title 8

CHAPTER 12—IMMIGRATION AND NATIONALITY

- *Subchapter II* is within Chapter 12

SUBCHAPTER II—IMMIGRATION

- *Part I* is within Subchapter II

PART I—SELECTION SYSTEM

Sec.
1151a. Repealed.
1157.   Annual admission of refugees and admission of emergency
        situation refugees [New].
        (a) Maximum number of admissions; increases for
            humanitarian concerns; allocations.
        (b) Determinations by President respecting number of
            admissions for humanitarian concerns.

- *Section 1158* is within Part I

1158.   Asylum procedure [New].
        (a) Establishment by Attorney General; coverage.

- *Subsection 1158(b)* is within Section 1158

        (b) Termination of asylum by Attorney General; cri-
            teria.
        (c) Status of spouse or child of alien granted asylum.

1159.   Adjustment of status of refugees [New].
        (a) Criteria and procedures applicable for admission
            as immigrant; effect of adjustment.
        (b) Maximum number of adjustments; recordkeep-
            ing.
        (c) Applicability of other Federal statutory require-
            ments.

SUBCHAPTER IV—REFUGEE ASSISTANCE
[NEW]

1521.   Office of Refugee Resettlement; establishment; appoint-
        ment of Director; functions.
1522.   Authorization for programs for domestic resettlement of
        and assistance to refugees.
        (a) Conditions and considerations.
        (b) Program of initial resettlement.
        (c) Project grants and contracts for services for refu-
            gees.

- The excerpt is on page 799 of the code

        (d) Assistance for refugee children.
        (e) Cash assistance and medical assistance for refu-
            gees.

Page 799

- *Subchapters* are smaller units within chapters
- *Chapters* are smaller units within titles
- *Titles* are smaller units within codes

In Figure 2, an excerpt from a table of contents in the *United States Code,* you can see that

- *Subsection 1158(b)* is within § 1158
- *Section 1158* is within Part I (there are no subparts in this excerpt)
- *Part I* is within Subchapter II
- *Subchapter II* is within Chapter 12
- *Chapter 12* is within Title 8
- *Title 8* is within the *United States Code.*

The excerpt is on page 799 of the code, but the page number is rarely of any significance. Statutes are identified and cited by subsection, title, etc., not by page number. (The symbol for a section is §; the plural is §§).

You need to understand the organizational structure of a code in order to see how any given statute fits into it. Assume you are reading a section that says, "Within this chapter, the word "license" means . . ." This language should alert you to the possibility that "license" may have a totally different meaning within some other chapter of the same code.

All of these units are *not* used in the citation of the statute in which you tell the reader where a certain statute is found in a law library. Often all that is needed for citation purposes is the section (or subsection) number, the title number, the name of the code (abbreviated), and the date of the edition of the code, e.g., 8 U.S.C. § 1185(c) (1976) for a federal statute. The page number on which the section is found in the code is never used in the citation. For the citation format to use when citing statutes in any code, consult *A Uniform System of Citation* (13th ed., 1981).

Also see Appendix B in this book for a list of standard statutory citation formats (p. 201).

Section B. Elements

Your analysis of a statute will usually focus on a particular section or subsection of the statute. For example:

> § 59(a). It is a defense to a prosecution under this subsection that the child was returned unharmed by the defendant prior to his arrest for the offense of taking the child in violation of a court order.

Assume that this is the statute that you are examining. It is in the smallest unit we have covered thus far—a subsection. But even this unit is too large for purposes of analysis; it must be further broken down. The smallest unit of any rule is what we will call an *element*.

An element is:

a. a portion of a rule, which

b. you identify on your own,

c. as one of the preconditions to the applicability of the entire rule, and which

d. can be conveniently analyzed separately from the other elements of the rule.

The skill of breaking down rules into elements can be valuable for many tasks in the law as demonstrated in Table 1.

This book focuses on element analysis as a technique of applying statutes although, as you can see, the concept of elements is significant throughout the legal system.

Note that *you* must perform the task of element identification. Occasionally you may come across statutes that readily lend themselves to an element breakdown because of grammatical structure, the presence of lists containing relatively brief items, etc. For most statutes, however, you will probably have to do some unraveling of the section or subsection in order to identify the appropriate elements.

A section or subsection of a statute may consist of a number of sentences within each paragraph, although it also may consist of one single-sentence paragraph. As a general guideline, you should treat each sentence as a separate rule for purposes of the element breakdown.

Table 1 The Value of Elements: Where they are Used in the Law	
Task	**How Elements are Used for this Task**
1. Preliminary analysis of a statute.	1. When you begin examining a statute, you first break it down into its elements. You then determine which elements are in contention. These elements become the basis of legal issues.
2. Preliminary analysis of any other rule of law, e.g., regulation, constitutional provision, ordinance, common law doctrine.	2. You approach these rules of law the same way as listed above for statutes.
3. Organizing a memorandum of law.	3. The memo is often organized around each element of the rules being applied, with emphasis given to those elements in contention. The elements are discussed in the memo one at a time.
4. Organizing an answer to a school essay examination question.	4. The answer is often organized around each element of the rules that the question asks you to apply, with emphasis given to those elements in contention.
5. Conducting a client interview.	5. The questions asked of the client are structured to elicit facts that are relevant to the elements of each rule that is potentially applicable in the case.
6. Conducting field investigation.	6. In the field you investigate facts that are relevant to the elements of each rule that is potentially applicable in the case.

Task—Continued	How Elements are Used for this Task—Continued
7. Drafting a complaint (the pleading that initiates the lawsuit).	7. Often the drafter of a complaint will allege those facts that support each element of the rules involved in the cause of action.
8. Conducting pretrial discovery (e.g., written interrogatories, depositions).	8. Questions asked during discovery are often structured to elicit facts that are relevant to the elements of each rule that is potentially applicable in the case.
9. Conducting direct examination and cross-examination at trial.	9. Questions are often asked of a witness on the stand that are relevant to each element of the rules involved in the case.

Our example of § 59(a) on p. 46 is a single-sentence paragraph. A possible formulation of the elements of this rule is as follows:

1. defense to a prosecution
2. under this subsection
3. child
4. was returned
5. unharmed
6. by the defendant
7. prior to his arrest for the offense of taking the child in violation of a court order

There is no magic to this formulation of the elements of § 59(a). It would not necessarily be an error to combine some of the elements above such as 1 and 2, or 4 and 5. Furthermore, it might even be appropriate to subdivide element 7 into two or more elements. The goal is to be as narrow as possible without losing context. Each element must be so structured that it can be conveniently discussed as a separate entity, at least initially.

Three special problem areas should be kept in mind when breaking rules into their elements:

1. Grammatical shorthand
2. "And"—express or implied
3. "Or"—express or implied

Grammatical Shorthand

When a statute contains a list, the drafter often uses grammatical shorthand to avoid repetition. For example, everything in the list may be modified by a single adjective, adverb, phrase, or clause, but the modifier may be given only once at the beginning or end of the list.

> § 35(h). The test of a petitioner's knowledge of the history and form of government of the United States must be given in the petitioner's native language.

Here we have two items in a list:

• history
• form of government

The phrase "of the United States" qualifies both of these items. The statute is referring to the history *of the United States,* and to the form of government *of the United States.* So too the word "knowledge" goes with both items: *knowledge* of history, and *knowledge* of the form of government. To avoid repetition, the drafter of the statute did not repeat the word "knowledge" or the phrase "of the United States." When you are stating elements, *be repetitive* when it is needed to clarify what words, phrases, and clauses go together:

1. the test
2. of a petitioner's
3. knowledge of the history of the United States, and
4. knowledge of the form of government of the United States
5. must be given in the petitioner's native language

Of course, it may not always be clear what language modifies or qualifies other language. The statute may have to be interpreted on this matter (p. 139). *One of the values of breaking down rules into their elements and phrasing them in this way is that you will force yourself to confront such ambiguity.*

"And"—Express or Implied

§ 173. The authorization must contain a description of the goods, their location, value, and approximate weight.

This statute contains a list in which the last item is preceded by an "and". There is an implied "and" between each of the other items in the list. The word "and" usually indicates additional requirements. Hence each item before and after all "and's" (express or implied) should go into its own separate element:

1. the authorization
2. must contain
3. a description of the goods *and*
4. a description of the location of the goods *and*
5. a description of the value of the goods *and*
6. the approximate weight of the goods

"Or"—Express or Implied

The word "or" sometimes poses problems. Occasionally the word is interpreted to mean "and". Most of the time, however, it refers to *alternative* rather than additional requirements (p. 140). When the word "or" means alternative requirements, all of the alternatives should be expressed within the *same* element. This should be done whether the "or" is expressly stated or implied. For example:

§ 28. So long as the will is properly executed, it can be written, printed, or typed.

1. will
2. properly executed
3.a. it can be written *or*

    b. it can be printed *or*

    c. it can be typed

The third element can be met by *any* of three alternatives. (Note that the word "or" is implied between "written" and "printed".)

> § 24.6(3). If an order to show cause has been issued, a district director, acting district director, assistant district director, or officer in charge of a branch office may cancel the order to show cause or, if the hearing has not commenced, terminate proceedings thereunder.

    1. order to show cause

    2. has been issued

    3.a. a district director *or*

      b. an acting district director *or*

      c. an assistant district director *or*

      d. an officer in charge of a branch office

    4.a. may cancel the order to show cause *or*

      b. if the hearing has not commenced, may terminate proceedings thereunder

There are four alternatives in the third element and two in the fourth. Some of the "or's" are expressed, others are implied; but they are all kept together within the element to which they belong.

Assignment # 13

Break down the following statutes into their elements:

a. The statute involved in the Caminetti case found on p. 2.

b. Section 404(a)(3)(A) found on p. 13.

c. Section 15.4(b) found on p. 29.

d. Section 242.9(a) Trial Attorney:

> (a) *Authority.* When an additional immigration officer is assigned to a proceedings under this part to perform the duties of a trial attorney, he shall present on behalf of the Government evidence material to the issues of deportability and any other

issues which may require disposition by the special inquiry officer. The trial attorney is authorized to appeal from a decision of the special inquiry officer pursuant to § 242.21 and to move for reopening or reconsideration pursuant to § 242.22.

e. § 2–302(1). Unconscionable Contract or Clause

(1) If the court as a matter of law finds the contract or any clause of the contract to have been unconscionable at the time it was made the court may refuse to enforce the contract, or it may enforce the remainder of the contract without the unconscionable clause, or it may so limit the application of any unconscionable clause as to avoid any unconscionable result.

The primary characteristic of an element is that its removal affects the applicability of the entire rule. If the facts of a case do not fit within *each* of the elements of the rule, the consequences of the entire rule cannot apply to the case. This does not mean, however, that the matching of facts and elements is a mechanical process. The words and phrases in the elements must still be defined and interpreted. Indeed, the value of analyzing rules through elements is that you have established a structure which should force you to raise questions of definition and interpretation for each element. The function of isolating elements will provide you with a checklist from which you can methodically ask such questions.

To demonstrate this, let us look more closely at § 59(a) and its elements:

§ 59(a). It is a defense to a prosecution under this subsection that the child was returned unharmed by the defendant prior to his arrest for the offense of taking the child in violation of a court order.

Elements:

1. defense to a prosecution
2. under this subsection
3. child
4. was returned
5. unharmed

6. by the defendant

7. prior to his arrest for the offense of taking the child in violation of a court order

We will examine each element at two levels: first, an initial reaction to the element based on a surface reading, and then a more probing reaction raising questions of definition and interpretation where warranted.

1. Defense to a prosecution

Section 59(a) appears to be a criminal statute. Someone must be charged with a crime who now wants to take advantage of the defense in § 59(a).

Questions: When does a "prosecution" begin? Can § 59(a) also apply to a civil case, e.g., a suit for damages, or a hearing to terminate the defendant from his or her employment for engaging in illegal conduct? Could the defense be used in a parole revocation hearing?

2. Under this subsection

The defense of § 59(a) applies to a prosecution under "this" subsection, and apparently not to prosecutions under any other subsections of the statute or to any other kind of prosecution that could be brought.

Questions: But is the defense *exclusive* to this subsection only? The statute does not explicitly say that the defense applies only to prosecutions under this subsection and to no other.

3. Child

The prosecution must involve a child.

Questions: What is a child? A person under 21? Under 18? Could a person be a "child" if he or she is 16 years old and married? Can a mentally incompetent adult be classified as a child? Is childhood determined by biological age only?

4. Was returned

The defense cannot be used unless the child is returned.

Questions: What does "returned" mean? Returned to whom? One of its natural parents? To its legal guardian? To the police? If the child goes to one of its relatives 25 miles away, has the child "returned"?

5. Unharmed

When the child has been returned, it must not have been harmed.

Questions: When does harm occur? What kind of harm? Physical harm only? *Any* physical harm or only *substantial* harm? What about psychological harm? Does trauma count? Who determines whether there has been harm? A doctor?

6. By the defendant

Even if the child has been returned, the defense cannot be used unless it is the defendant who returns the child.

Questions: Does the defendant have to bring the child back in person? What if the defendant asks a friend to bring the child back? What if the defendant gives the police information on where the child can be found and the police return the child? What if the defendant tells the child to "get out" and the child returns on its own? In these situations, has the child been returned "by the defendant." ?

7. Prior to his arrest for the offense of taking the child in violation of a court order

Timing is important under the statute. The return must occur before the defendant is arrested for taking the child in violation of a court order.

Questions: Can the defendant use the defense if he or she returns the child after he or she is arrested on another charge (e.g., theft), but before the arrest for taking the child in violation of a court order?   What happens if the court order is later found to have been invalid by an appellate court?

Note the method of approach: isolate and challenge. First, separate out the elements.   Analyze them one at a time, at least initially.   Make a quick reading of the language to determine what it appears to be saying.   Then, and most importantly, challenge the language.   Ask questions about it. Note any ambiguity.   Wonder aloud about the scope of the language.   Ask yourself about the definitions of everything in the element.   Later we will study the techniques of answering such questions through the canons of construction, legislative history, court interpretations, etc.   But before you identify the answer, you must identify the question!   This is done by refusing to take statutory language at face value.   In short, it is done by challenging the language of the statute through its elements.

Section C. Identifying and Phrasing Issues of Statutory Construction

A legal issue is a question of law which arises when an attempt is made to apply a rule to certain facts.   If the rule is a statute, then the legal issue will involve the applicability of the statute to the facts.

Most statutory issues center on the interpretation of a small number of words or phrases in a section or subsection of a statute.   While it is quite possible for an issue to involve several statutes or an entire statutory scheme, the vast majority of statutory issues are much narrower.   The method of identifying the latter kind of issue is as follows:

i. Break the statute into its elements

ii. Examine the facts of the case involving the statute

iii. In light of these facts, identify each element that is probably in contention

iv. Phrase a separate legal issue for each element in contention

v. The issue should consist of three components:

    a. a brief quote from the element in contention

    b. the essential facts that raise the question of the applicability of this language in the element

    c. the section or subsection number where this element is located

Later we will examine the identification of more complex kinds of legal issues.

Example:

> § 1403(b). Employees of the city government entering Building C must show their pass to a guard on duty.

> *Elements:*

> 1. employees of the city government

> 2. entering Building C

> 3. must show their pass

> 4. to a guard on duty

Assume that the facts of the case involve Smith and the Deputy Mayor. Smith is a former city employee who is about to go into Building C. The Deputy Mayor of the city happens to be walking out of the building when she meets Smith at the front door. She asks Smith for his pass. He ignores her and walks in.

The legal issue is whether Smith has violated § 1403(b). This, however, is a shorthand statement of the issue. A more accurate phrasing would result from connecting the facts to the elements in contention. Elements 2 and 3 are not in contention. No one is going to dispute that Smith entered Building C and did not show a pass. But elements 1 and 4 are in contention: does "employees" include former employees, and does a "guard" include the Deputy Mayor? Based on these two elements in contention, two separate issues can be more formally identified:

> *First Issue:* When a former city employee enters Building C and does not show a pass, does he violate § 1403(b) which requires that passes be shown by "employees of the city government"?

Alternative phrasing of first issue: When § 1403(b) requires that "employees of the city government" show their passes on entering Building C, does the word "employees" include former employees?

Second Issue: When a former city employee enters Building C and does not show a pass as requested by the Deputy Mayor, has this former employee violated § 1403(b) which requires a showing of a pass "to a guard on duty"?

Alternate phrasing of the second issue: When § 1403(b) states that employees of the city government must show their pass upon entering Building C "to a guard on duty", can the Deputy Mayor be considered a "guard on duty"?

Note that each issue contains all three components for an issue: a quote from the element in contention, the essential facts that raise some ambiguity in this quote, and the section or subsection number where the element is found. Other portions of the statute are also mentioned in the issue to provide context, but the focus is on the quoted language since this is what must be interpreted or construed within the issue. Either of the alternative phrasings of an issue can be used. The first phrasing begins with the essential facts, and the second begins with the element in contention.

Another Example:

§ 43.7. The taking of photographs and the operation of tape recorders in the courtroom or its environs and radio or television broadcasting in the courtroom or its environs during the progress of or in connection with judicial proceedings, whether or not the court is actually in session, is prohibited.

Elements:

1.a. the taking of photographs, *or*

  b. the operation of tape recorders, *or*

  c. radio broadcasting, *or*

  d. television broadcasting

2.a. in the courtroom, *or*

  b. its environs

3.a. during the progress of judicial proceedings whether or not the court is actually in session, *or*

b. in connection with judicial proceedings whether or not the court is actually in session

4. is prohibited

Note that in this statement of elements, the first "and" in § 43.7 is interpreted as an "or". Operating a tape recorder is prohibited even if no photographs are taken during the tape recording, and vice versa. The legislature arguably intended *alternatives.* If, however, the first element is in contention on this point, further analysis would be needed before drawing any final conclusions.

> *Facts:* The criminal trial of Jane Robertson has just begun. The judge is on the bench. Defense counsel, however, is late. WBZ–TV, on the steps of the courthouse, films defense counsel dashing into the courthouse.
>
> *Issue:* When a TV station on the steps of the courthouse films defense counsel going to a trial that is in progress, has the station violated § 43.7 which prohibits television broadcasting within the "environs" of the courtroom?

Another issue might be explored: does "broadcasting" mean live action? If so, we would have to find out whether the WBZ–TV film was shown live.

Assignment # 14

Phrase the legal issue or issues based on the statute in the *Caminetti* case on p. 1.

Assignment # 15

Phrase the legal issue or issues from Assignment 10 on § 15.4(b) and the facts of that Assignment, p. 29.

Assignment # 16

Phrase the legal issue or issues from Assignment 11 on § 19 and the facts of that Assignment, p. 30.

Assignment # 17

Phrase the legal issue or issues from Assignment 12 on § 1.119–1 and the facts of that Assignment, p. 30.

Assignment # 18

Phrase the legal issue or issues based on § 31.2 and the following facts:

Statute: § 31.2. Investigation

After the filing of any complaint, the Board shall serve, within 15 days of said filing, a copy thereof upon the respondent, and upon all persons it deems to be necessary parties; and shall make investigation in connection therewith.

Facts: On March 5 (Wednesday) Smith files a complaint at the Board against Brown. On March 21 (Friday) the Board serves a copy of the complaint upon Brown, the respondent. On March 21, the Board begins its investigation of Brown. Brown claims that the service was after the 15 days of filing and therefore, the Board has lost its power to investigate under § 31.2.

Assignment # 19

Phrase the legal issue or issues based on § 75(d) and the following facts:

Statute: § 75(d). Tender of Payment

Any buyer making tender of full payment to a seller when or after it is due is discharged to the extent of all subsequent liability for interest, costs, and attorney's fees.

Facts: X has offered to sell Y some goods. Both agree to the deal. X brings the goods to Y and asks for payment. Y says, "I'll give you the money if you agree to sell me the same amount of goods for the same price next month." X refuses. Y, therefore, does not give X the money. X takes the goods back and sues Y for breach of contract, and under § 75(d), claims interest, costs, and attorney's fees (to represent X in the suit against Y). Y argues that § 75(d) does not apply.

Assignment # 20

Phrase the legal issue or issues based on § 408 and the following facts:

Statute: § 408. Be it enacted by the Senate and House of Representatives of the United States of America in Congress assembled, that from and after the passage of this Act it shall be unlawful for any person, company, partnership or corporation, in any manner whatsoever, to prepay the transportation, or any way assist or encourage the importation or migration of any alien or aliens, any foreigner or foreigners, into the United States, its territories or the District of Columbia, under contract or agreement, parol or special, express or implied, made previous to the importation or migration of such alien or aliens, foreigner or foreigners, to perform labor or service of any kind in the United States, its territories or the District of Columbia.

Facts: The Church of the Holy Trinity is a corporation, duly organized and incorporated in the state of New York. E. Walpole Warren, prior to September, was an alien residing in England. In that month, the church made a contract with him to come to New York and serve as rector and pastor. Pursuant to this contract, he came to New York. The church is charged with violating § 408. The church claims that it does not apply.

In the discussion thus far we have concentrated on issues where only one statute was involved. As indicated, such issues are the ones most frequently raised. More complex issues can arise in a number of situations:

(a) Whether One Statute is Consistent with Another Statute Occasionally the claim is made that two statutes conflict with each other. For example, a statute gives an agency the power to investigate something. The agency conducts an investigation of a company under this statute. The company claims that the agency acted illegally because a different statute gives another agency exclusive jurisdiction to investigate the matter involved. The issue is whether the two statutes are consistent. Which agency has the authority to investigate? Only one of them? Both? The phrasing of the issue would consist of brief quotes from the elements of both statutes that are in contention plus the essential facts in the company's case that raise the ambiguity in these elements. For example:

> *Issue:* Does the State Waterway Commission have the exclusive authority to investigate "all shoreline accidents" under § 268, or does the Bureau of Transportation Safety have this authority under § 118.5 which requires the Bureau to make recommendations "growing out of safety hazards on the roads, highways, and other modes of transportation"?

(b) Whether a Statute is Consistent with the Constitution Statutes must be validly based on the constitution (p. 151). The claim is sometimes made that a statute violates the constitution. For example:

> *Issue:* Does a state violate the "due process clause" of the Fourteenth Amendment when it provides in § 43 of its Corrections Code that "no hearings shall be held prior to the transfer of a prisoner from one penal institution to another within the state"?

(c) Whether a Regulation is Consistent with a Statute Agency regulations must be validly based on statutes. One of the strategies of a citizen who feels aggrieved by a regulation is to claim that the regulation violates the statute because the agency misread the statute (p. 155). For example:

> *Issue:* Is § 79 of the Environmental Service Department's regulations valid when it imposes "two week license suspensions for trucking companies that violate the pollution standards", in view of § 5528(r) of the Health Code which provides that this Department can impose "any sanction other than one that would directly or indirectly lead to the cessation of business of any company authorized to do business in this state"?

(d) Whether a Statute Changes the Common Law As we have already seen, the legislature can always change the common law (p. 7). It is sometimes difficult to determine, however, whether the legislature intended to make this change, and, if so, what the extent of the change is (p. 7). For example:

> *Issue:* When a man lies to a woman to whom he is engaged on whether he had ever been married before, can she sue him in a common law action for fraud even though the legislature in § 10 has "abolished all contract actions growing out of marriage engagements other than one involving the return of engagement gifts"?

None of these more complex kinds of statutory issues are substantially different from the single-statute issue discussed earlier. All are based on elements in contention and specific facts from the case that require these elements to be interpreted. The only difference is that more than one rule is involved in the issue. The methods of identifying and phrasing the issue (discussed in this chapter) and of resolving the issue (discussed in other chapters) are the same.

Section D. Memos and Other Kinds of Legal Writing

A memorandum of law is simply a written explanation of how law(s) apply to the facts of a current case. Occasionally a memorandum will be sent to a judge or administrative agency in order to try to persuade the recipient to make a decision favorable to the party on whose behalf the writer is advocating. Most memos, however, are for "in-house" distribution only. They are written to help the office prepare strategy and give advice. On the basis of these interoffice memos, other kinds of legal writing are often prepared. For example:

• A letter to the client in nontechnical language providing the status of the law and legal advice

- A letter to an official at an administrative agency requesting certain action or inaction
- An appellate brief which is a highly technical document submitted to a court of appeals after the trial is over in which the court is asked to approve or disapprove what the lower court has done in the litigation

The starting point leading to these kinds of legal writing is the interoffice memorandum of law. One of its most important characteristics is, or should be, objectivity. It must present the strengths *and* weaknesses of the client's case so that the senior members of the office can make intelligent decisions based upon all aspects of the law. The memo will certainly attempt to show how the law can be interpreted in the light most favorable to the client, but it must go beyond this level. The memo also must try to anticipate what the strongest arguments of the *opponent* will be. Such arguments must be presented with precision and honesty. When this is done, the reader of the memo within the office will be in the best position to design *realistic* strategy.

Not all supervisors agree on the preferred structure of the interoffice memorandum of law. The following are the most common features that are required:

1. HEADING

At the top of the page you state the kind of document you are writing (interoffice memorandum of law). You then list:

- The person to whom the memo is addressed
- The name of the author of the memo
- The date the memo was prepared
- The client's name and opponent
- The office file number of the case
- The court docket number if the case has already been filed in court
- A very brief subject-matter entry (following the notation "RE:") in which you state what the memo is about

2. STATEMENT OF THE ASSIGNMENT

It is a good idea early in the memo to provide an explicit statement of what your supervisor has asked you to do in the memo.

3. STATEMENT OF THE LEGAL ISSUE(S)

The issues should be stated comprehensively. For statutory issues, provide the three-part issue discussed earlier: a brief quote from the element in contention, the essential facts which are the basis of this contention, and the section or subsection number where the element is found (p. 56).

4. STATEMENT OF THE FACTS

Here all the relevant facts of the case are provided. Include only those facts which will be analyzed in the body of the memo.

5. DISCUSSION OR ANALYSIS

Here you present the law and explain its applicability to the facts, i.e., you try to answer the issues. For memos that require the interpretation of statutes, a suggested organizational structure is as follows:

• State the entire section or subsection of the statute that you will be analyzing. Include only what must be discussed in the memo. If the section or subsection is long, you may want to place it in an appendix to the memo. If you are going to discuss more than one section or subsection, treat them separately in different parts of the memo unless they must be discussed together.

• Break the section or subsection down into its elements. List each element separately. You can omit any element or portion of an element which is obviously irrelevant to the case under analysis.

• Briefly tell the reader which elements will be in contention and why. In effect, you are telling the reader why you have phrased the issue(s) the way you did earlier in the memo.

• Go through each element you have identified, one at a time, spending most of your time on the elements that are in contention.

• For the elements not in contention, simply tell the reader why you think there will not be any dispute about them, e.g., you anticipate that both sides probably will agree that the facts clearly support the applicability or nonapplicability of the element.

• For the elements in contention, go through the analytical steps that will be discussed in this book, e.g., use the canons of construction such as the plain meaning rule; discuss court opinions that have interpreted the statute, if any; discuss regulations and administrative decisions that have interpreted the statute, if any; discuss the legislative history of the statute, if available; discuss scholarly interpretation of the statute, if any. (See the summary chart on methodology, p. 37.)

• Give opposing viewpoints for the elements in contention. Try to anticipate how the other side will interpret these elements, e.g., what counterarguments will the other side probably make based on its use of the canons of construction, court opinions, legislative history, etc.

6. CONCLUSION

Give your personal opinion on which side has the better arguments. Do not state any new arguments in the conclusion. Simply state your own perspective on the strengths and weaknesses of the arguments you have made above.

7. RECOMMENDATIONS

State any specific recommendations that you feel are appropriate in view of the analysis and conclusion that you have provided, e.g., further facts should be investigated, further research should be undertaken, a letter should be written to the agency involved, the case should be litigated or settled.

8. APPENDIX

At the end of the memo, include items that you referred to in the memo, e.g., photographs, statistical tables, the full text of statutes.

What follows is an interoffice memorandum of law that conforms with the recommended structure. Assume that the supervisor wants this memorandum within a few hours after it is given to you. You are asked to provide a preliminary analysis of the statute. Hence, at this point there has been no time to do any research on the statute, although you should indicate what research you think will be appropriate.

INTEROFFICE MEMORANDUM OF LAW

TO: Mary Jones, Esq.

FROM: Tim Farrell

DATE: March 13, 1984

CASE: Department of Sanitation v. Jim Donaldson

OFFICE FILE NUMBER: 84-114

DOCKET NUMBER: (none at this time; no action has been filed)

RE: Whether Donaldson has violated § 17

A. ASSIGNMENT

You have asked me to do a preliminary analysis of § 17 [23 State Code Ann. § 17 (1980)] to assess whether our client, Jim Donaldson, has violated this statute. No research on the statute has been undertaken thus far, but I will indicate where such research might be helpful.

B. LEGAL ISSUE

When a government employee is asked to rent a car for his agency, but uses the car for personal business before he signs the lease, has this employee violated § 17 which prohibits the use of ''property leased to the government'' for nonofficial purposes?

C. FACTS

Jim Donaldson is a government employee who works for the State Department of Sanitation. On February 12, 1984, he is asked by his supervisor, Fred Jackson, to rent a car for the agency in order to make an important delivery. At the ABC Car Rental Company, Donaldson is shown several cars available for rental. He asks the manager if he could test drive one of the cars for about 15 minutes before making a decision. The manager agrees. Donaldson then drives the car to his home in the area, picks up a TV, and takes it to his sister's home. When he returns, he tells the manager that he wants to rent the car for his agency. He signs the lease and takes the car to the agency where it is used for the important delivery. The supervisor, however, finds out about the trip that Donaldson made to his sister with the TV. He is charged with a violation of § 17. Since he is a new employee at the agency, he is fearful that he might lose his job.

D. ANALYSIS

Donaldson is charged with violating 23 State Code Ann. § 17 (1980) which provides as follows:

§ 17. Use of Government Property

An employee of any state agency shall not directly or indirectly use government property of any kind, including property leased to the government, for other than officially approved activities.

To establish a violation of this statute, the following must be shown:

  (1) An employee of a state agency
  (2)(a) directly uses government property of any kind including property leased to the government or
  (b) indirectly uses government property of any kind including property leased to the government
  (3) for other than officially approved purposes

The main problem in this case will be the second element.

(1) Employee of a state agency

Donaldson works for the State Department of Sanitation, which is clearly a ''state agency'' under the statute.

(2) Use of property leased to the government

The central issue is whether Donaldson directly used property leased to the government. (The rented car was not owned by the government. Hence it was not ''government property''. And Donaldson acted ''directly'' rather than ''indirectly'' such as by causing someone else to drive the car.) There should be no dispute that when Donaldson drove the car to his sister, he directly used property. But was it property leased to the government''?

Donaldson's best argument is that when he made the trip to his sister, he had not yet signed the lease. The car did not become property leased to the government until after he returned from his sister's house. No costs were incurred by the government because of the test drive. Rental payments would not begin until the car is rented through the signing of the lease.

The supervisor, on the other hand, would argue that the statute should not be interpreted narrowly. The overall goal of the legislature in passing § 17 was to avoid misuse of government resources. Public employees should not take advantage of their position for private gain. To do so would be a violation of the public trust. This is what Donaldson did. While on the government payroll, he obtained access to a car and used it for a private trip. It is not clear from the facts whether the manager of the ABC Rental Company knew that Donaldson was going to rent the car for a government agency when he received permission to take the test drive. This should be checked. If the manager did know, then the likelihood is that Donaldson used the fact that he was a government employee to obtain the permission. He held himself out as a reliable individual because of the nature of his employment.

The phrase ''property leased to the government'' should be interpreted broadly to include both the signing of the lease and the necessary steps leading up to the signing. Everyone would agree that Donaldson would have violated the statute if he had made the TV trip moments after he signed the lease. It is illogical to argue that there is no violation if he made the trip moments before he signed the lease. Given the purpose of § 17, the legislature could not have intended such a result.

I have not yet checked whether there are any court opinions or agency regulations interpreting § 17 on this point.

Nor have I researched the legislative history of the statute. All this should be done soon.

(3) Officially Approved Purposes

Nothing in the facts indicates that Donaldson's supervisor, Fred Jackson, gave him any authorization to make the TV trip. Even if Jackson had authorized the trip, it would probably not be ''officially'' approved since the trip was not for official (i.e., public) business.

E. CONCLUSION

Donaldson has the stronger argument based on the language of the statute. The property simply was not ''leased'' at the time he made the TV trip. I must admit, however, that the agency has some very good points in its favor. Unlike Donaldson's technical argument, the agency's position is grounded in common sense. Yet on balance, Donaldson's argument should prevail.

F. RECOMMENDATIONS

Some further investigation is needed. We should find out whether the ABC Rental Company manager knew that Donaldson was a government employee at the time he asked for the test drive. In addition, legal research should be undertaken to find out if any court opinions and agency regulations exist on the statute. A check into the legislative history of § 17 also is needed.

Finally, I recommend that we send a letter to Donaldson's supervisor, Fred Jackson, explaining our position. I have attached a draft of such a letter for your signature in the event you deem this action appropriate.

There is one matter that I have not addressed in this memo. Donaldson is concerned that he might lose his job over this incident. Assuming for the moment that he did violate § 17, it is not at all clear that termination would be an appropriate sanction. The statute is silent on this point. Let me know if you want me to research this issue.

Farrell, Grote, & Schweitzer
Attorneys at Law
724 Central Plaza Place
West Union, Ohio 45328
513–363–7159

March 15, 1984

Frederick Jackson
Field Supervisor
Department of Sanitation
3416 34th St. NW
West Union, Ohio 45328

RE: James Donaldson
84–114

Dear Mr. Jackson:

Our firm represents Mr. James Donaldson. As you know, some question has arisen as to Mr. Donaldson's use of a car prior to the time he was asked to rent it for your agency on February 12, 1984. Our understanding is that he was asked to go to the ABC Car Rental Company in order to rent a car for a certain delivery that was needed at your agency, and that he did so satisfactorily.

Your agency became responsible for the car at the moment Mr. Donaldson signed

the lease for the car rental. It is
clear that no personal use could be made
of the car from that moment. It is also
clear that no such personal use occurred.
What happened prior to the time the lease
was signed is not relevant. The governing statute (§ 17) is quite explicit.
It forbids nonofficial use of property
''leased'' to the government. Such use
did not occur in this case. No one has
questioned Mr. Donaldson's performance of
his duty once he ''leased'' the car.

    If additional clarification is needed,
we would be happy to discuss this matter
with you further.

                        Sincerely,

                        Mary Jones, Esq.

   wps: MJ

Assignment # 21

Smith is an ex-convict on parole. He goes to a church bingo
game. While filling out his score card, he is arrested for
possession of gambling records. Smith claims that the following statute applies to his case, but the prosecutor
disagrees:

   48 State Code Ann. § 225.25 (1979)

   In any prosecution for possession of gambling records it is a
   defense that the writing, paper, instrument or article possessed
   by the defendant was neither used nor intended to be used in
   the operation or promotion of a book-making scheme or enterprise, or in the operation, promotion or playing of a lottery or
   policy scheme or enterprise.

Your supervisor asks you to prepare a preliminary memorandum of law on the applicability of § 225.25 to the case of
Smith, a client of the office where you work. Do no legal

research at this time, although you should point out what kind of research might be helpful. After you complete the memo, draft a letter to the prosecutor stating the position of your office on the applicability of § 225.25. Your ultimate aim is to try to convince the prosecutor to drop the case. The letter will be signed by your supervisor. (You can make up the names and addresses of the people involved as well as any dates that you need.)

Assignment # 22

Draft a preliminary memorandum of law applying 8 U.S.C. § 408 (1920) to the facts of E. Walpole Warren involved in Assignment # 20 (p. 60). Do not do any legal research at this time, although you should point out what kind of research might be helpful. You work for the law firm that represents the Church of the Holy Trinity. After you complete the memo, draft a letter to the Bureau of Immigration which is seeking to deport Reverend Warren. In the letter you want to present arguments against such action. The letter will be signed by your supervisor. (You can make up the names and addresses of the people involved as well as any dates that you need.)

Chapter Five

The Plain Meaning Rule, the Mischief Rule, and the Golden Rule

Section A. The Plain Meaning Rule

> It is elementary that the meaning of a statute must, in the first instance, be sought in the language in which . . . [it] is framed, and if that is plain, . . . the sole function of the courts is to enforce it according to its terms. Caminetti v. United States, 242 U.S. 470, 485, 37 S.Ct. 192, 194, 61 L.Ed. 442 (1916).

This principle operates as a rule of caution: courts must not change a statute under the guise of interpreting it. If the language of a statute has a "plain meaning," it must be followed. The starting point of analysis is the "four corners" of the statute, i.e., its language. If there is no ambiguity within this text, then the court's "sole function" is to "enforce it according to its terms."

As we have seen, however, there are problems in applying the plain meaning rule (p. 3). The meaning of language is derived from its context. While words do have ordinary and natural dictionary definitions, the meaning of words cannot be conclusively established in the abstract. The word "minor" might mean *eighteen or over* in one context, but *twenty-*

one or over in another. The word "competent" might mean *having a high degree of skill* in one context, but *having the minimal ability to care for one's self* in another. The context of statutory language includes the purpose the legislature had in passing the statute, its legislative history, the relationship of the statute to other statutes, etc. To obtain this context, you obviously must go "outside" the four corners of the statute.

Section B. The Mischief Rule

If a statute is to make sense, it must be read in the light of some assumed purpose. A statute merely declaring a rule, with no purpose or objective, is nonsense. K. Llewellyn, *Remarks on the Theory of Appellate Decision and the Rules or Canons About How Statutes are to be Construed,* 3 Vand.L.Rev. 395, 400 (1950).

Minn.Stat. § 645.16 (1980):

The object of all interpretation and construction of laws is to ascertain and effectuate the intention of the legislature. Every law shall be construed, if possible, to give effect to all its provisions.

When the words of a law in their application to an existing situation are clear and free from all ambiguity, the letter of the law shall not be disregarded under the pretext of pursuing the spirit.

When the words of a law are not explicit, the intention of the legislature may be ascertained by considering, among other matters:

(1) The occasion and necessity for the law;

(2) The circumstances under which it was enacted;

(3) The mischief to be remedied;

(4) The object to be attained;

.   .   .

The mischief rule is one technique of identifying legislative intent. Ask yourself why the legislature passed the statute. What was its objective? What need prompted it? What evil or mischief was it trying to correct? Then assess whether answers to such questions can be helpful in determining what the legislature meant by certain words or phrases in the statute as applied to a given set of facts before you.

Assume that § 100 of the worker's compensation code provides that there shall be recovery for an "accident arising out of employment". Joe Smith is an employee at a local factory. While on the job, his co-worker, Bob Richardson, suddenly throws a wrench at Joe because the latter refuses to join a union. Joe is severely injured and applies for worker's compensation benefits. Has an "accident" occurred under § 100? What is an "accident"? Is it a mishap that unexpectedly occurs without anyone being at fault? Or does it have a broader meaning: any unexpected occurrence regardless of fault?

Assume further that the worker's compensation code was enacted by the legislature in order to provide a quick method of compensation for workers injured on the job. Before the code came into existence, workers had to go through a long court procedure in order to obtain compensation. Because of certain defenses easily available to employers (such as assumption of the risk), many workers recovered nothing. The statute abolished some of these defenses and provided a method of recovery in an administrative agency where the delays and technicalities of a court trial were eliminated.

The question is whether this legislative purpose helps us decide which definition of "accident" the legislature intended. Arguably it does. The legislature was trying to help the worker. The evil or mischief that the legislature wanted to remedy was the large number of employees who receive no compensation for worker-related injuries or who have to go through an unduly burdensome court proceeding in order to collect anything. Joe Smith seems to fall within the category of individuals the legislature was trying to benefit. A worker who is injured by someone's fault is as much in need of the protection of the worker's compensation statute as a worker who is injured through no one's fault. Hence, one can argue, in view of the purpose of the statute, that the legislature intended the broader definition of "accident" since this definition will best effectuate the remedy that the legislature sought to put in place.

How do you determine the legislative purpose of a statute? How do you identify the evil or mischief it was trying to remedy? There is often no clear answer. Some guidelines include:

• The preamble of the statute. At the beginning of the statute, there may be a statement of purpose. Often, however, this statement is too general to be of much help.

• The legislative history of the statute (p. 97). Committee reports and floor debates often cover the purpose of the statute.

• The four corners of the statute itself. It may be possible to identify the purpose of the statute from what the legislature has said throughout the statute.

• Court opinions interpreting the statute. Courts often discuss the purpose the legislature had in passing the statute. They reach this conclusion primarily through the above three guidelines.

• Agency interpretations of the statute in regulations and administrative decisions (p. 194).

• Scholarly comment on the statute (p. 40). Such comment will draw on all five of the above guidelines.

Assignment # 23

In 1970 there is a serious housing crisis in the city. Many tenants are living in apartments that are hazardous to their health and safety. To solve this problem, the legislature passes a Housing Code under which tenants living in such conditions can complain to the Housing Authority about landlords who fail to maintain their buildings properly. Section 57 provides that "it shall be a violation of this code for any landlord to rent an apartment in a condition that is hazardous to health or that is dangerous in any way." Edward Yuma is a landlord in the city. He rents an apartment to Fred Stanton. The apartment is rat-infested and is in a state of serious disrepair. Stanton complains to the landlord about these conditions. The latter does nothing. Stanton then stops paying his rent. When the landlord sues for back rent, Stanton defends by claiming that the lease is void due to the landlord's violation of § 57. Stanton believes that he should not have to pay rent until the conditions in the apartment are corrected. The Housing Code is silent on whether this defense is available to a tenant. Make an argument in support of Stanton's position on the basis of your perception of the legislative purpose behind the statute.

Assignment # 24

Apply § 11.1 to the facts below. Where appropriate, determine what you think the legislative purpose of § 11.1 is and how this purpose might be helpful in interpreting the statute.

Facts: The ABC Truck Co. is charged with violating § 11.1(a)(1). The Company has a policy of asking applicants for employment to work for no pay for a period of ten days. If the company likes the performance of the applicant, he or she is hired. Harrison applies for a job. He agrees to the ten-day trial period without pay. On the fifth day, he is told to leave the premises permanently because the manager found out that Harrison lives in a district that overwhelmingly voted Democratic in the last election. Harrison feels that the company's action violates § 11.1(a)(1).

Statute: § 11.1

(a) General: It shall be an unlawful discriminatory practice to do any of the following acts, wholly or partially for a discriminatory reason based on the race, color, religion, national origin, sex, age, marital status, sexual orientation, family responsibilities, physical handicap, or political preference of any individual:

(1) By an employer:

discharge any individual, or otherwise to discriminate against any individual, with respect to his compensation terms, conditions, or privileges of employment, including promotion; or to limit, segregate, or classify his employees in any way, which would deprive or tend to deprive any individual of employment opportunities, or otherwise adversely affect his status as an employee.

Assignment # 25

It is illegal under § 36 "to drive, operate, or park any mode of transportation on the sidewalk in this city." What do you think the legislative purpose of § 36 is? How, if at all, does this purpose help to resolve the question of whether § 36 was violated in the following circumstances:

a. Tom rides his unicycle on the sidewalk.

b. Bill roller-skates on the sidewalk.

c. Mary rides a skate board on the sidewalk.

d. Linda pushes her Pinto on the sidewalk and leaves it there. There is no motor in the car.

e. To avoid hitting another car, Rich swerves his car quickly to the right and momentarily drives two feet onto the curb.

Assignment # 26

Section 12 requires "employers to provide a safe place in which employees can work while repairing structures at the workplace." An employee is injured while washing the walls of the company plant. Has § 12 been violated? In your analysis include arguments based on your perception of the legislative purpose of § 12.

Assignment # 27

Section 343 provides that the death penalty can be imposed on any person who commits murder "against a peace officer while such officer is engaged in the performance of his official duty." Mary murders Smith who is an undercover narcotics agent dressed in street clothes at the time of the murder. Can Mary receive the death sentence? In your analysis include arguments based on your perception of the legislative purpose of § 343.

Section C. The Golden Rule

> Yet the plain meaning rule has limitations. It has long been recognized that the literal meaning of a statute will not be followed when it produces absurd results. District of Columbia National Bank v. District of Columbia, 348 F.2d 808, 810 (D.C. Cir. 1965).

The golden rule is another aid in identifying legislative intent. Or, more accurately, it inclines us to *avoid* an interpretation of a statute to which an application of the plain meaning rule would otherwise lead us. We must presume that the legislature did not intend any interpretation of the statute that would lead to absurd or ridiculous consequences, no matter how "plain" the meaning of the statute *appears* to be.

For example, § 68 provides that "all gymnasiums shall be closed at midnight every day of the week." Holiday Gymnasium, Inc. closes its facilities at midnight and then reopens them two minutes later. The statute requires that the gym "shall be closed at midnight." Holiday argues that it has complied with this requirement since its gym *is* closed at midnight. Using a literal interpretation of the statute, Holiday is correct. But this obviously leads to an absurd result. The legislature could not have intended to allow a gym to avoid the statute by closing down at the designated time and then reopening moments later. To avoid this absurdity, we interpret § 68 to mean closing down at midnight *and remaining closed until the following regular business day*.

Assignment # 28

Diane is intoxicated. While driving her car in this state, she hears a funny noise in the rear of her car. She stops the car in the middle of the road. With the motor running, she goes to the back of the car to inspect. At this moment, a police officer sees her for the first time. When the officer stops and discovers that she is intoxicated, he asks her to take a breath test. She refuses. Section 78 gives the police the right to take such a test whenever "there is reasonable cause to believe that someone driving a car is intoxicated." What argument can she make to support the position that she does not have to take the breath test? Apply the golden rule to this argument. Would it make any difference if the officer's first contact with her occurred while she was vomiting next to her car which she had just parked?

Assignment # 29

Section 56(r) gives the Superior Court "jurisdiction to hear all cases involving any contract dispute regardless of the amount in controversy." David Crawford is a prostitute. A client who had agreed to pay him a certain price now refuses to pay for the services rendered. David sues this client in Superior Court for breach of contract. Assume that he can prove all of his allegations, e.g., the price agreed upon, the nonpayment. Does the golden rule apply?

Assignment # 30

Section 368 provides that "no boxing matches shall be held in any bar, restaurant, or other public facility." The Gabriel Bar conducts a nightly contest in which a patron is challenged to box the owner in front of all the other patrons in a ring specially built in the center of the bar. Gabriel wants to continue these events. Can it be done? What approaches do you think Gabriel could take in order to avoid the prohibition of § 368? Apply the golden rule to each of these approaches.

Chapter Six

Canons of Construction: Customs in the Use of Language

Section A. The Canons are not Canons

> The so-called rules of interpretation are not rules that automatically reach results, but [are] ways of attuning the mind to a vision comparable to that possessed by the legislature. J. Landis, *A Note on "Statutory Interpretation,"* 43 Harv.L.Rev. 886, 892 (1930).

Rules of interpretation are commonly called "canons of construction." In fact, however, they are not rules or laws in the technical sense of this word. No canon in and of itself ever conclusively resolves a dispute over the meaning of a statute. No court is required to apply a canon. The canons are merely generalizations about the use of language; they are customs of writing. When drafters of statutes or any writers sit down to communicate their thoughts, they *usually* follow these customs. Hence, when we attempt to interpret their writing, we can try to use these customs as *guidelines* in identifying meaning. Given the nature of the canons, the following principle must govern our use of them:

> The canons are guidelines suggesting a certain meaning of statutory language which can be adopted unless it is clear that the legislature intended a different meaning.

Some of the canons have imposing Latin names which give the impression that you deviate from them at your peril. But again they are no more than maxims or customs of writing and composition in general, and of legislative writing and composition in particular. In some situations the canons will be of no help; indeed, different canons might even suggest opposite interpretations of the same statute. You use the canons for what they are worth: *potential* guidelines to probable or possible meaning.

In the preceding chapter we discussed the plain meaning rule, the mischief rule, and the golden rule. These are also canons of construction—perhaps the most important ones available. Hence they were given separate attention. As we shall see, some of them must be examined again in relationship to several of the canons to be covered in this chapter:

- Expressio unius est exclusio alterius
- Noscitur a sociis
- Ejusdem generis
- In pari materia
- Terms of art

Section B. Expressio Unius Est Exclusio Alterius

John, just before he dies, writes a will in which he leaves all of his property "to my good friend George." Both John and George would be quite surprised to learn that Bill claims that John left his property to *Bill*. John expressly said that the property was to go to George. *By implication*, John was "saying" that it was *not* to go to Bill or to anyone other than John. This is the effect of the rule, expressio unius est exclusio alterius: the mention of one thing is the exclusion of another. When we are examining statutory language, or any other kind of writing, common sense suggests that when the writer specifically mentions one item, he or she by implication intends to exclude some other item. As interpreters of the language, we must honor this intent to exclude unless it is otherwise clear that this was not the intent.

Example:

Facts: Irene is a used car dealer. One day she brings a rifle to work. As an ex-hunter, she no longer needs the rifle and wants to sell it. After making a sale of a used car to a customer, she asks him if he would like to buy a rifle for $100. He is very interested but wants some time to think about it. Irene agrees and signs a statement in which she says, "I offer to sell you the rifle for $100. This offer will terminate in three days." Two days after Irene signed this statement, the customer comes in with the $100 and says that he would like to buy the rifle. Irene responds by saying that she has changed her mind. "The rifle is no longer for sale." The customer then sues Irene under § 26(a) and § 26(b).

Statutes: § 26(a). An offer by a merchant to buy or sell goods in a signed writing which by its terms gives assurance that it will be held open is not revocable during the time stated.

§ 26(b). "Merchant" means a person who deals in goods of the kind involved in the transaction.

Did Irene violate § 26(a) by failing to keep her offer open during the time stated in writing? It depends upon whether she is a "merchant". The statute says a "merchant" is someone "who deals in goods of the kind involved in the transaction". Irene is a merchant as to used cars. She deals in used cars. There is no indication that she deals in rifles. The matter involving the rifle appears to be an isolated transaction. The legislature expressly said that a merchant was someone who deals in goods of the kind involved in the transaction. The transaction here is the attempted sale of the rifle as to which Irene is arguably not a merchant. By implication, Irene argues, the legislature did not intend to cover her offer to sell the rifle: expressio unius est exclusio alterius. By implication, the legislature did not intend to cover people who do not deal in goods of the kind since it expressly *included* people who do so. The statute is exclusive as to who is a merchant.

This is the effect of applying the canon, expressio unius est exclusio alterius. But the analysis does not stop here. The canon is but a point of departure. Other aids of interpretation must also be used. Suppose, for example, that the customer does some research into the legislative history of § 26 (p. 97) and discovers support for the view that the word "merchant" should be given a broader interpretation: any person who sells *any* goods to the public as part of a commercial transaction. Perhaps the mischief rule (p. 76) also supports this conclusion. The purpose of the statute may have been to protect citizens from merchants regardless of how many times the merchant may try to sell a certain product. This interpretation may also be supported by other canons.

Again, *all* methods of discovering legislative intent and meaning must be explored. No one method or technique can be examined in isolation. It should not trouble you that they do not always point in the same direction. Litigation may be needed to resolve the dispute. A court will have to decide which approach is most persuasive in interpreting the statute. The job of the advocate, particularly in the preparation of a memorandum of law (p. 62), is to lay out all of the options and to analyze the case from the perspective of both sides of the controversy. This requires using all resources and aids available.

Assignment # 31

Tom has been invited to Fred's house for a cup of coffee. While pouring the coffee, the pot explodes in Tom's face. Fred purchased the coffee pot one week ago from the XYZ Appliance Center. Section 37 provides that "an implied warranty of merchantability is extended by every seller of goods to buyers in the normal course of business." It can be clearly established that the coffee pot was defective; it was not merchantable. Tom sues the XYZ Appliance Center for violating § 37. What result?

Assignment # 32

In the following three situations, determine whether § 23 has been violated:

a. Johnson is a full-time judge in the state. He fails to file any registration statement. Has he violated § 23?

b. Smith is an attorney admitted to practice in the state. He files his registration statement on time, and it contains all the required information. At the bottom of his statement he adds the following comment, "I wish to go on record as being offended by having to submit this registration statement. It is a bother and an invasion of my privacy." The clerk refuses to accept this registration statement and sends it back to him. Has Smith violated § 23? Has the clerk violated § 23?

c. The attorney hands the registration statement to one of the judges of the court mentioned in § 23. Has the attorney violated § 23?

§ 23. Periodic Registration of Attorneys

Every attorney admitted to practice in this state or who regularly engages in the practice of law within this state as house counsel to corporations or other entities, as counsel for governmental agencies, or otherwise, shall, on or before January 31, of every year, or within three (3) months of the effective date of these rules, or within three (3) months of his becoming subject to these rules by admission or otherwise, file with the clerk of this court, on forms to be provided by the clerk, a registration statement setting forth his date of admission to this court, or, if not admitted in this court, the date of admission and the court to which he is admitted, his current residence and office addresses, and such other information as the court may from time to time direct. In addition to such registration statement, every attorney shall file a supplemental statement with the clerk showing any change in the information previously submitted within thirty (30) days of such change.

Assignment # 33

a. John and Mary are each 17 years old. John's parents consent to their marriage. Mary's mother consents. Mary's father does not consent. Can they be validly married under § 57–1–6?

b. Ed is 17 years old. He goes through a marriage ceremony on January 10, 1976 with Susan who is 16 years old. On January 5, 1976, Susan gave birth to a child by Ed. They lied about their age because they knew their parents would not consent. Is their marriage valid under § 57–1–6? If not, can they now be married validly?

> § 57–1–6. Restrictions on marriage of minors.—A. No person authorized by the laws of this state to celebrate marriages shall knowingly unite in marriage:
>
>> (1) any person under the age of eighteen (18) years without the consent of their parents or guardians; or
>>
>> (2) any person under the age of sixteen (16) years with or without the consent of their parents or guardians.
>
> B. The children's or family court division of the district court may authorize the marriage of persons under the ages stated in subsection A where the female is under the age of consent and is pregnant if the marriage would not be incestuous.

Section C. Noscitur a Sociis

This canon cautions us against taking words out of context. Words in a sentence can have a certain meaning *because* of their association with other words in the sentence or paragraph. This is the effect of the canon, noscitur a sociis: something is known by its associates.

Example:

> *Facts:* The Parker Envelope Company owns a three-story building where its 40 employees work. In one of the rooms on the second story the company keeps numerous boxes of supplies. There are boxes along the walls, in the aisles, in front of the entrance door, etc. The company is charged with violating § 93 because of the condition of this room.
>
> *Statute:* § 93. Commercial enterprises employing ten or more workers must keep floors, steps, stairs, and gangways free from obstruction.

The boxes in the second-story room clearly constitute obstructions. But are they on "floors" within the meaning of

§ 93? The answer would be "yes" according to the common dictionary definition of this word. In context, however, the word may have a different meaning.

Closely examine the other words in the statute: steps, stairs, and gangways. What do they all have in common? They each designate areas where workers regularly *travel* into and out of parts of the building; they are passageways or parts of passageways. Arguably, when the legislature used the word "floors," it intended only those floors which workers regularly used as passageways. If so, this would not include floors in a storage room. We arrive at this possible meaning by reason of the words associated with the word "floors" in the statute.

Of course, all of the other aids of construction must be used in order to assess the validity of this interpretation of § 93. It may be that a court will reject the use of the maxim, noscitur a sociis, if it finds no ambiguity in the statute. The court may take the position that storage room floors are floors, and that it strains the imagination to hold otherwise:

> That a word may be known by the company it keeps is . . . not an invariable rule, for the word may have a character of its own not to be submerged by its association. Rules of statutory construction are to be invoked as aids to the ascertainment of the meaning or application of words otherwise obscure or doubtful. They have no place . . . except in the domain of ambiguity. Russell Motor Car Co. v. United States, 261 U.S. 514, 519, 43 S.Ct. 428, 430, 67 L.Ed. 778 (1923).

Assignment # 34

Ralph Oliver is a World War II veteran. As a memento of his military career, he keeps a rifle on the wall which he captured from the enemy. When Ralph's grandchildren visit, he often gives them a demonstration of how the rifle works. He feels that he should not have to pay the tax imposed by § 2.44: "A $5 tax shall be collected for the possession of each and every rifle, fishing boat, snowmobile, and diving apparatus." Does he owe the tax?

Section D. Ejusdem Generis

One of the most common and troublesome problems of statutory construction is the interpretation of a general catch-all phrase following a list of specific items:

"Hunting, fishing, horse racing, *or other public events.*"

"Oil, gas, *and other minerals.*"

"Hotel, motel, rooming unit, dwelling unit, *or building used for sleeping purposes.*"

What is the meaning of the general phrase? Does it add anything to the specifics mentioned? If not, then the phrase is surplusage. We must presume that the legislature intended to give meaning to every part of the statute. On the other hand, if we interpret the general phrase too literally, it could potentially include a vast number of items.

Ejusdem generis ("of the same kind") is a technique of interpreting such general phrases. It is a version of the broader maxim, noscitur a sociis. According to ejusdem generis, the general phrase is limited in meaning to the same category or classification found within the specific items in the list. "Other public events" in the first statute above, for example, might mean any *outdoor sporting* venture such as water skiing or field hockey. It would not include showing a motion picture in a traditional theater even though the latter would be a "public event" if this phrase were taken literally.

The rule of ejusdem generis conforms to common-sense thinking patterns. If Tom told a relative to use Tom's funds to purchase "food, clothing, and whatever else you need," Tom would be quite surprised to learn that the relative took a world cruise at Tom's expense. One reason for the rule (when legislation is involved) is that the drafter of the language must be taken to have inserted the general words *in case* something which ought to have been included among the specifically enumerated items has been omitted; a further reason for the rule is that, if the general words were intended to have their ordinary meaning, the specific enumeration would be pointless. R. Cross, *Statutory Interpretation* 116 (1976).

To apply ejusdem generis, carefully examine all the specific items in the statute. Then determine what, if anything, they have in common. Can you identify a classification or categorization that is common to all of these specifics? If so, you then attribute this same classification or categorization as the boundary line of the general phrase.

As with any canon, however, caution is needed in its application. A contrary interpretation might be called for when you examine the legislative history of the statute (p. 97) or apply the mischief rule (p. 76), the golden rule (p. 81), or any other aid. While the rule of ejusdem generis

> is a well-established and useful one, it is, like other canons of statutory construction, only an aid to the ascertainment of the true meaning of the statute. It is neither final nor exclusive. To ascertain the meaning of the words of a statute, they may be submitted to the test of all appropriate canons of statutory construction, of which the rule of ejusdem generis is only one. If, upon a consideration of the context and the objects sought to be attained and of the act as a whole, it adequately appears that the general words were not used in the restricted sense suggested by the rule, we must give effect to the conclusion afforded by the wider view in order that the will of the Legislature shall not fail. Helvering v. Stockholms Enskilda Bank, 293 U.S. 84, 89, 55 S.Ct. 50, 52, 79 L.Ed. 211 (1934).

Assignment # 35

In each of the following problems you will find a statute and one or more sets of facts. Determine whether the statute applies to the facts.

a. Statute: § 13. A deduction can be taken for losses that arise from fire, storm, shipwreck, or other casualty.

Facts:

i. Smith's car is demolished in a street collision.

ii. Dr. Tory cannot collect a $250 bill from a patient.

iii. Jones loses a watch in a burglary.

iv. Jackson's fence is destroyed when a neighbor's tree falls on the fence. The neighbor was carelessly cutting down her tree.

v. An arsonist destroys Simpson's home.

b. Statute: § 31.71. An officer on active duty may be permitted to set up a special account within the district financial unit consisting of a part or all of his monthly pay for the payment of insurance premiums, union dues, the purchase of securities of the federal government, or other proper purposes.

Facts: A police officer on active duty wants to set up a special account within the district financial unit.

i. Twenty percent of his monthly pay is to be sent to the City Revenue Department to purchase city bonds.

ii. An amount to be determined by an arbitrator is to be sent to his ex-wife as alimony.

c. Statute: § 705(g). It shall be unlawful to possess a dagger, dirk, knife, razor, switch blade, stilleto, or other dangerous weapon.

Facts: On Davis's day off, the police find an ice pick in his glove compartment. Davis is an ex-convict.

d. Statute: § 88. An injunction can be obtained against any person who falsely claims to be the inventor of a product by circular, advertisement, or otherwise.

Facts: George writes a letter to Sam falsely stating that he (George) invented the walk-man radio.

e. Statute: § 63(d). No obscene or other improper literature can be sent in the mail.

Facts: Bill sends Helen a letter in which he falsely claims that she is a thief.

f. Statute: § 21. The Commission has jurisdiction over theaters, opera houses, arenas, and other places of amusement.

Facts: In a local drugstore there are seven coin-operated video games. The store claims that the commission has no jurisdiction over it.

g. Statute: § 100. Civil rights shall not be denied at inns, hotels, restaurants, theaters, and other places of public accommodation.

Facts: Charles refuses to serve Episcopalians at his bootblacking stand on the corner of 5th and Vine Streets.

h. Statute: § 608.7. Evidence of abandonment shall include exposure of the child in a street, field, or other place with the intent to leave the child there indefinitely.

Facts: Roger took his infant child to the church rectory. When no one was looking, he left the child in a corner of the hallway and ran out.

Section E. In Pari Materia

Statutes in pari materia ("on the same subject") are to be interpreted together even though they may have been passed at different times. While there may be differences between the statutes, courts will attempt to interpret them as consistent with each other. If this is not possible, then the more recent or the more particular statute will usually control:

> [A]lthough two statutes relating to the same general subject matter should be read together and harmonized, if possible, with a view to giving effect to a consistent legislative policy, nevertheless, to the extent that statutes are inconsistent, the later statute, which deals with the same subject matter in a particular way, will prevail over an earlier statute of a more general nature, and the latter statute will be regarded as an exception to or qualification of the earlier general statute. City of Flat River v. Mackley, 212 S.W.2d 462, 466 (Mo.App.1948).

The inclination to try to harmonize the two statutes is based on the common-sense assumption that when the legislature enacted statutes on the same topic, it most likely intended

that they be consistent with each other even though the statutes contain no reference to each other.

Suppose, for example, that § 23 of the *General* Elections
Law specifically provides that candidates for the general
election "must be listed on the ballot with only one party
designation," but that no such prohibition exists in § 589 of
the *Primary* Election Law. The two statutes are on the same
subject—in pari materia. They both cover the law of elections. The court will try to harmonize the two statutes. For
example, it could read the multiple-party prohibition of the
general election law into the primary election law. This conclusion may be supported by the mischief rule (p. 76) in
view of the legislative purpose of the two statutes. The
golden rule (p. 81), may also support this interpretation since
it is arguably unlikely that the legislature intended the absurd result of allowing a candidate to be nominated in the
primary as a Republican *and* a Democrat, but then forcing the
candidate to be disqualified for the general election unless
one of these party designations is selected.

As indicated, however, where the statutes are irreconcila-
ble, particular statutes are preferred over general statutes and
later statutes over earlier ones—unless an intent to the contrary can be established.

Section F. Terms of Art

Legislation when not expressed in technical terms is addressed
to the common run of men and is therefore to be understood
according to the sense of the thing, as the ordinary man has a
right to rely on ordinary words addressed to him. Addison v.
Holly Hill Fruit Products, Inc., 322 U.S. 607, 618, 64 S.Ct. 1215,
1221, 88 L.Ed. 1488 (1944), (Justice Frankfurter).

In the construction of the laws and statutes of this state, both
civil and criminal, words and phrases shall be read and construed with their context, and shall, unless inconsistent with
the manifest intent of the legislature or unless another or dif-

ferent meaning is expressly indicated, be given their generally accepted meaning, according to the approved usage of the language. Technical words and phrases, and words and phrases having a special or accepted meaning in the law, shall be construed in accordance with such technical or special and accepted meaning. N.J. Stat.Ann. § 1:1–1 (West, 1939).

Statutes are written to be understood. Statutory language is to be interpreted according to the ordinary and common meaning of the words used *unless it is clear that the legislature intended a different meaning.* Words and phrases that have a special or technical meaning are called terms of art. These can be scientific terms, accounting terms, commercial terms, or legal terms. Often the statute will have a separate definitions section which defines terms as they are to be used in the statute. If such sections do not exist, then other evidence must be introduced as to their meaning, particularly for scientific and trade terminology.

Many legal terms are never defined in a statute. For example: consideration, jurisdiction, estate, interest, premises, proximate cause. A great deal of litigation has occurred and will continue to occur over the meaning of such terms either in the abstract or as applied to a given set of facts.

When a definitions section does not exist, how do you determine whether the legislature intended certain words to be understood according to their common meanings or as terms of art? All of the aids of interpretation must be used. The subject matter and context of the statute may provide clues. The mischief rule (p. 76), the golden rule (p. 81), legislative history (p. 97), and the other canons of construction will often be helpful. Court and agency interpretations (p. 37) must always be checked.

The safest course is to assume that a technical meaning was intended until you establish otherwise through the above techniques.

Chapter Seven

The Use of Legislative History in the Interpretation of Statutes

Section A. Advocacy Objectives in Arguments Based on Legislative History

As we shall see, there is a good deal of controversy surrounding the use of legislative history as an aid in the interpretation of statutes. Some argue that such use is unfair and inherently inconclusive. Others take the position that it violates common sense to ignore the historical context of a statute in the search for its meaning. Before examining this controversy, we need to identify the reasons that advocates resort to arguments based on legislative history and the relationship between such arguments and the more traditional approaches to interpreting statutes.

> *Problem:* In 1975 the state legislature enacts the Liquor Control Act which provides in § 33 that "Liquor shall not be sold on Sunday or on any day on which a local, state, or federal election is being held." The Fairfax Country Club claims that § 33 does not apply to the sale of liquor on Sunday or on Election Day *by membership clubs*; it applies only to bars that provide service to any customers that come in off the street. The question, therefore, is whether the legislature intended to include membership clubs within the restrictions of § 33. The State

97

Liquor Board says that it did. The Fairfax Country Club argues that it did not.

In this case, several different kinds of proceedings can occur in which the interpretation of § 33 becomes the main issue. The State Licensing Agency may hold a hearing on the revocation of the liquor license of the Fairfax Country Club for violating § 33. The result of this hearing may be appealed in court. Or the state may be able to go directly to court to seek an injunction against the Club in order to force it to comply with § 33.

The advocates for both sides have the responsibility of marshaling arguments in favor of their respective positions. This will include traditional approaches such as:

• Examining the "four corners" of the statute itself (§ 33) to determine the meaning of the words used

• Examining the preamble or purpose clause of this statute, if any, to help determine the purpose of the statute—what it was trying to accomplish

• Examining definitions sections in the statute, if any, to determine the meaning of words used by the legislature in § 33

• Examining court opinions that have interpreted § 33, if any

• Examining administrative regulations that implement § 33, if any

• Examining administrative decisions that have interpreted § 33, if any

In addition, both sides will research the legislative history of § 33. An advocate who fails to do so runs the risk of being unprepared. It is true that some courts tend to be antagonistic toward the use of legislative history for reasons that we will examine later. The advocate, however, cannot respond to this antagonism by ignoring legislative history; the antagonism must be handled by presenting the legislative history in such a way that the court cannot ignore it.

An advocate has two objectives while researching the legislative history of a statute:

1. To determine whether the specific facts currently in controversy were ever discussed by the legislature while it was considering the proposed statute

2. To determine the broad or narrow purpose that prompted the legislature to enact the proposed statute and to assess whether this purpose sheds any light on the specific facts currently in controversy

For example, when the legislature was considering § 33, was there any mention of country or membership clubs in the governor's message, in committee reports, in floor debates, etc.? If so, what was said about them? What was said about the purpose of § 33? Why was it enacted? What evil or mischief was it designed to combat? Was the legislature opposed to liquor on moral grounds? Did it want to reduce rowdyism that comes from the overuse of liquor? Did it want to encourage citizens to go to church on Sunday and to vote on election day? Were there complaints made to the legislature about the use of liquor by certain groups in the community? Answers to such questions might be helpful in formulating arguments on the meaning and scope of § 33. The advocate for the Fairfax Country Club will try to demonstrate that the legislature had a narrow objective when it enacted § 33: to prevent neighborhood rowdyism at establishments that serve only liquor. The legislature, therefore, was not trying to regulate the more moderate kind of drinking that normally takes place at membership clubs where food and liquor are often served together. The opponent, on the other hand, will argue that the legislature had a broader purpose in enacting § 33: to decrease the consumption of liquor by all citizens on certain days. The legislature, therefore, did not intend to exclude drinking at a membership club.

Arguments based on legislative history must be related to the more traditional arguments mentioned earlier (e.g., examining the four corners of the statute, preamble, definitions sections, court opinions, administrative regulations and decisions). The advocate must show that the arguments based on legislative history:

• Are consistent with and *reinforce* the interpretation of the statute derived from the more traditional sources *or*

• Are inconsistent with but *more persuasive* than the arguments derived from the more traditional sources *or*

• Are the *only arguments available* because the traditional sources are not helpful in resolving the current controversy

In short, while legislative history cannot be ignored, it must be presented in the context of other kinds of arguments.

Section B.   The Historical Context of a Statute

On p. 104 Figure 3 outlines the steps that a bill goes through before it becomes a statute. The chart assumes that the legislature considering the bill is bicameral, i.e., consists of two houses. The two houses are referred to as the House and the Senate. (In some legislatures the houses may have different names, e.g., the Assembly and the Senate.) Legislatures with only one house are called unicameral. There are very few state legislatures that are unicameral. Local legislatures, however, such as city councils, are often unicameral.

The process of enactment can involve six major stages:

1. Proposal
2. Initial committee consideration
3. Floor debate
4. Conference committee consideration
5. Floor debate
6. Signature of the chief executive

The legislative history of a statute is what occurs at each of these stages. When an advocate "combs" the legislative history, he or she will be looking for anything that might be relevant to a current controversy concerning the interpretation of a statute, e.g., whether the legislature intended to include membership clubs in the exclusions of § 33.

1. PROPOSAL

The idea for a statute can come from many sources. The chief executive of the government (e.g., president, governor) may initiate the process by sending the legislature a message in which the reasons for a proposed law are stated. Frequently an administrative agency has made a study of a problem which is the impetus for the proposal. The agency usually will be the entity with responsibility for administrating the proposal if it is enacted into law.

The bar association may prepare a report to the legislature calling for the new legislation. The legislature or chief executive may have established a special commission to study the need for changes in the law and to propose changes where appropriate. The commission might consist of members of the legislature and outside experts. In some states there are ongoing Law Revision Commissions that frequently make proposals for legislation. In many areas there are Councils of Government made up of neighboring governments. Such Councils often study problems and propose legislative changes. The National Conference of Commissioners on Uniform State Laws is an organization with members from each state. The Conference makes proposals to the state legislatures for the enactment of laws where it deems uniformity to be desirable.

Finally, the idea for the legislation may be generated within the legislature itself. An individual legislator can always propose a bill. One or both houses of the legislature may have established an investigating committee to examine a problem and propose legislation where needed.

2. INITIAL COMMITTEE CONSIDERATION

The next step is for a member of the legislature to introduce the bill. This introduction is usually accompanied by a statement as to why the bill should be enacted. The bill may be introduced in only one of the houses or in both houses simultaneously by a member of each house. If the latter option is not used, then the bill often will be intro-

duced in the other house after it has been considered by the
first house. As bills are introduced, they are assigned a con-
secutive number (e.g., S 250 is the 250th bill introduced in
the Senate during the current session; HR 1753 is the 1753rd
bill introduced in the House of Representatives during the
current session).

Once the bill is introduced, it follows a similar procedure
in each house. The bill is sent to the committee with responsibility over the subject matter of the bill, e.g., a bill to
change the criminal law might go to the Judiciary Committee. The initial draft of the bill might be considered by this
committee or by one of its subcommittees. Hearings are
held. Citizens and public officials give testimony for or
against the bill. In some legislatures this testimony is transcribed so that a word-for-word record is made available.
Legislators often propose amendments to the bill which are
voted upon by the committee. The committee then issues a
report summarizing why the bill is needed and what its major provisions are. If there is disagreement on the committee, a minority report often is prepared.

3. FLOOR DEBATE

The bill with its accompanying report(s) then goes to the
floor of the house of which the committee is a part. The bill
is debated by the full house. During the debate, which may
be transcribed, questions are asked by members as to the
meaning of certain provisions in the bill: what is covered
and what is not. Amendments often are made from the
floor and voted upon.

4. CONFERENCE COMMITTEE CONSIDERATION

Since both houses act independently of each other in considering the bill, it is rare that they will both produce the exact
same bill. Inevitably, the amendment process leads to different versions of the proposed law. To resolve these differences, a conference committee is established consisting of
key members of both houses, e.g., the chairpersons of the
committees that considered the bill, the members who intro-

duced or sponsored the bill initially. A compromise is attempted in this committee. Amendments are considered and a final report of the conference committee is issued. Dissenting members of the committee might prepare a minority report. The majority report summarizes the major terms of the compromise and explains why it should be enacted by each house.

5. FLOOR DEBATE

The conference committee compromise then goes back to the floor of each house where more debate, explanations, and amendments are considered. Again, everything may be transcribed. If both houses pass the same version of the bill, usually by majority vote, it goes to the chief executive.

6. CHIEF EXECUTIVE

The bill becomes law if the chief executive signs it. When it is signed, the chief executive sometimes will make a statement as to why this action is being taken. If he or she vetos or refuses to sign the bill, it goes back to the legislature, often with an explanation as to why it is being disapproved. If a designated number of legislators (usually two-thirds in each house still vote in favor of the bill, it becomes law over the objection of the chief executive.

Section C. The Controversy Over the Use of Legislative History

Several interrelated reasons account for the controversy surrounding the use of legislative history as an aid in the interpretation of a statute:

1. Availability and Cost
2. Reliability
3. Manipulation
4. Overuse

FIGURE 3. The Legislative History of a Statute—How a Bill Becomes a Law

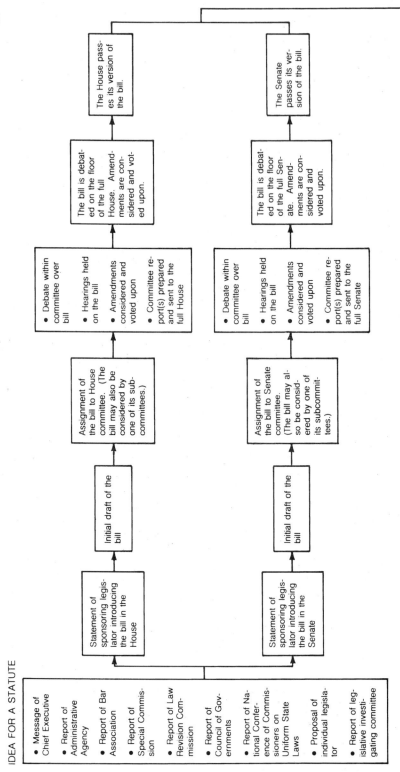

IDEA FOR A STATUTE

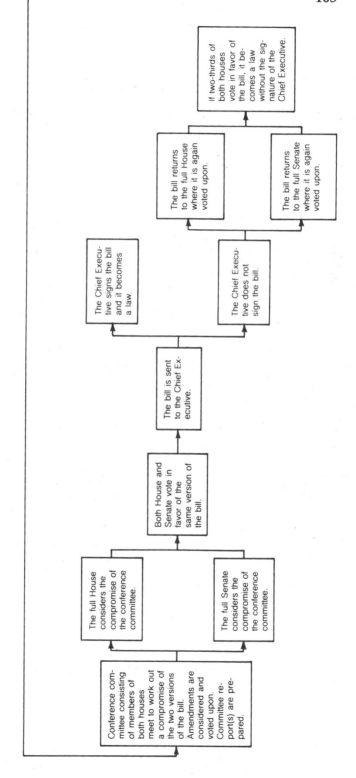

1. AVAILABILITY AND COST

As you can see from the preceding section, a statute can have a great deal of legislative history. Given the vast numbers of statutes in existence, the task of collecting and researching their legislative histories can be enormous. Justice Jackson suggested that this impracticality raises a basic question of fairness:

> Laws are intended for all of our people to live by; and the people go to law offices to learn what their rights under those laws are. [Controversies exist which affect] every little merchant in many States. Aside from a few offices in the larger cities, the materials of legislative history are not available to the lawyer who can afford neither the cost of acquisition, the cost of housing, or the cost of repeatedly examining the whole congressional history. Moreover, if he could, he would not know any way of anticipating what would impress enough members of the Court to be controlling. Schwegmann Bros. v. Calvert Distillers Corp., 341 U.S. 384, 396, 71 S.Ct. 745, 751, 95 L.Ed. 684 (1951), concurring opinion.

In spite of the increased availability in recent years of the documents of legislative history, they are still generally inaccessible, particularly for state statutes. It is much easier to undertake such research for federal statutes than for state statutes. Yet even for the former, the cost of the research can be substantial. An advocate may have to examine thousands of pages in a variety of books. Few clients can afford this kind of service. In the next section of this chapter, we will explore some of the main books and techniques of researching the legislative history of a statute. Knowing about these books and techniques, however, does not diminish the point made by Justice Jackson. A comprehensive examination of the documents of legislative history can be an expensive and time-consuming task. The records that are needed may not be equally available to everyone.

2. RELIABILITY

Assume that in a particular case there are no problems of availability and cost—you are able to collect and study the entire legislative history of a statute. At this point, another problem arises. How reliable is the data that you are examining? Information from legislative history is reliable to the extent you can establish that:

• The information was considered by the legislature and

• The information accurately reflects what the legislature ultimately did

Suppose that Senator Smith sends a letter to a constituent explaining the meaning of a bill and why he or she is supporting it. In a broad sense, this letter is part of the legislative history of the statute that came from the bill, but the letter is totally unreliable. There is no rational way of determining whether the legislature *as a whole* considered the letter and acted in accordance with its contents. The strong likelihood is that neither occurred. Would it make any difference if this letter was also printed in the official record or journal of the legislature while the bill was being considered? Probably not. A great deal is printed during the course of a legislature's consideration of a bill. Much of it is considered junk. According to some commentators, research into legislative history consists in large measure of rummaging through "the ashcans of the legislative process." C. Curtis, *It's Your Law* 52 (1954).

Suppose, however, that this same legislator is speaking to another legislator on the floor of the Senate during a debate on the bill:

Senator SMITH: The purpose of this bill is to phase the government out of the business of operating a railroad. It establishes an Interim Management Council which will run the affairs of the railroad until such time as private capital can take over complete management.

Senator THOMAS: Senator, am I correct in understanding that the bill currently before the Senate applies only to those railroad facilities in which the government acquired an interest prior to 1974?

Senator SMITH: The senator is indeed correct.

Here we have an exchange between two legislators during a floor debate on the bill. Presumably there are other legislators listening to this debate so that we are on safer ground in concluding that the legislature considered what they had to say. It would be helpful to know who Senator Smith is. Is he the sponsor of the bill or the chairperson of the committee that initially considered it? If so, his comments are likely to be given more weight. Courts are more inclined to conclude that the legislature considered what he had to say and, if the bill was enacted, that his comments accurately reflect what the legislature intended. The views of legislators who did not have such a key role in sheparding the bill through the legislature are usually given less weight. Such views are considered less reliable in deciphering the meaning of the statute.

Yet it must be remembered that this piece of legislative history focuses only on the views of individual legislators. We can *never* be certain that these views accurately record what hundreds of legislators tried to do in passing the bill. This is so even if the individual legislator in question actually wrote the bill. According to Lord Halsbury:

> [I]n construing a statute I believe the worst person to construe it is the person who is responsible for its drafting. He is very much disposed to confuse what he intended to do with the effect of the language which in fact has been employed. At the time he drafted the statute, at all events, he may have been under the impression that he had given full effect to what was intended, but he may be mistaken . . . . Hilder v. Dexter, [1902] A.C. 474, 477.

While there is some merit to this skepticism which English courts have toward the use of legislative history, American courts have not gone this far. As indicated, our courts do give weight to the statements of legislators who had an important role in passing the bill.

Perhaps the most reliable documents of legislative history are the committee reports that are written after the committee holds hearings on the bill and debates amendments thereto. These reports often have two main components.

First, they state the purpose of the bill: what it is trying to accomplish. They will often include discussions of prior law on the subject of the bill (including court opinions). Such discussion is usually provided as background on why the bill is needed. Second, the reports contain a section-by-section summary of the bill. It is sometimes claimed that many legislators do *not* read the technical language of the bill itself. Instead, they rely on the more readable summaries of the bill contained in the committee reports.

Some committees also print transcripts of the testimony of witnesses who appear before the committee on the bill. However, given the diversity of this testimony and the early stage at which it is provided in the legislative process, it is rarely relied upon as indicative of what the legislature intended when it passed the bill.

What about special commission studies, messages of the chief executive, and reports of councils of government and of commissioners on uniform laws? To what extent can their proposals for legislation be relied upon to determine the legislative intent of the bills that are enacted? These proposals, of course, are also made early in the process, and a great deal may happen between the time of proposal and the date of enactment. The reliability of these initiating documents may depend on whether the language of the bill that was enacted is the same as the language of the bill that was proposed by the commission, chief executive, council, etc. If the language is the same or very similar, then the accompanying study, message, or report of these groups is generally accorded great weight in determining legislative intent.

In summary, therefore, the following are considered the most reliable components of legislative history in the interpretation of statutes:

- Committee reports
- Statements of legislators who sponsored the bill or who chaired committees that favorably considered it
- Studies, reports, and messages of bodies that initially proposed the bill

While the use of any legislative history still remains controversial, the above components are most frequently relied
upon.

3. MANIPULATION

Perhaps the most cynical explanation for the reluctance of
some courts to use legislative history is the tendency of legislators and legislative staff members to "plant" statements
and commentary in the legislative history for the sole reason
of influencing later interpretation of the statute:

> But the intentions of some member of the subcommittee staff,
> buried in a report . . . are not the statute and do not nec-
> essarily represent the intentions of Congress. We all know the
> propensity of people who cannot persuade Congress to include
> a provision in the statute to insert comments favorable to their
> position in the legislative history in the hopes of persuading a
> court later on that what they say is what Congress had in mind.
> Application of Commonwealth Edison Co. for a Permit for
> Dresden Unit 3, No. 70–21, Illinois Pollution Control Board,
> 3/3/71, reported in 5 CCH Atom.En.Rep.Par. 16,613 at 22638.
> See Murphy, A., *Old Maxims Never Die: The "Plain-Meaning Rule"
> and Statutory Interpretation in the "Modern" Federal Courts*, 75 Col.L.
> Rev. 1299, 1312–3, n. 100 (1975).

Under this view, statements and commentary in the legislative history are no more reliable than what someone says on
the telephone when he or she knows that there is a wiretap
on the phone! Assume that a legislator wants to enact a law
that prevents an agency from regulating a particular practice.
For various political reasons, the legislator cannot collect
enough votes from colleagues to support this provision.
Hence the language that is to be voted upon by the legislature is intentionally left vague or general. The legislator
then instructs a committee staff member to state in the committee report that the bill is intended to accomplish the specific objective that the legislator had in mind initially. Also,
this legislator might conveniently arrange for another legislator to ask a question on the floor during debate on the
meaning of the vague or general language in the bill. A re-

sponse is then made for the record which is in accord with what the legislator was not able to insert in the bill itself. Such manipulative maneuvers are common enough to cast doubt on the reliability of legislative history in the interpretation of statutes.

W. MOORHEAD, "A CONGRESSMAN LOOKS AT THE PLANNED COLLOQUY AND ITS EFFECT ON THE INTERPRETATION OF STATUTES"

45 American Bar Association Journal 1314 (Dec.1959).*

Because of the complexity of modern federal legislation, courts, in construing legislative intent, have resorted to legislative history including the record of debates on the floor of Congress.

Mindful of this judicial scrutiny, legislators of today have used the opportunity of debate to achieve legislative goals which might otherwise be unattainable. Indeed, by the use of the "friendly colloquy", two men may be able to legislate more effectively than all of Congress.

This type of colloquy is presented in the form of a friendly exchange of questions and answers about the pending legislation between members, one of whom is usually a member of the committee from which the legislation emanated. This seeming repartee is not accidental. In fact it is just the opposite. It has been carefully planned by the parties for the express purpose of providing a legislative interpretation of a statutory provision which might otherwise be differently interpreted.

The need for the type of explanation provided by such a colloquy may arise for various reasons. It may be used to overcome legal, parliamentary or political obstacles.

As every legislative draftsman knows, it is difficult, if not impossible, to avoid ambiguities and cover every contingency

---

* W. Moorhead was a Member of Congress. Reprinted with permission from American Bar Association Journal.

with legislative language. Sometimes such legal obstacles may be overcome by an explicit statement in the committee report, but often it is desirable to clarify the purpose and intent of the statute during debate. This is particularly true where an ambiguity is not discovered until after the committee report has been filed.

Parliamentary obstacles can be overcome by use of the planned colloquy. Rule XIX of the Rules of Procedure of the House of Representatives prohibits amendments in the third degree. A substitute bill is considered as an amendment. If, for example, after a substitute bill has been adopted, an amendment is proposed, this amendment is not subject to further amendment. If further clarification is necessary, resort must be had to colloquy.

For reasons of strategy, proponents of a particular bill may want to oppose all amendments. They may fear that if one amendment is adopted it will open the door to further amendments. In such a situation, however, the proponents might be willing to participate in a friendly colloquy.

In other situations proponents of a bill will stage a planned colloquy to give a construction to a bill which will, they hope, win over opponents of the legislation.

Perhaps the most interesting and controversial use of the colloquy to overcome political obstacles arises when it is engaged in for the purpose of establishing a meaning and intent to legislation which could not have been accomplished by direct language in the statute. Many if not most bills are controversial to some degree, and often it may be desirable when drafting a bill to couch provisions in innocuous language in order to minimize possible objections during committee consideration. Naturally, however, the proponents of a particular viewpoint would like to insure that their interpretation be the accepted one. The friendly colloquy on the floor during debate can serve well in this situation. Acquiescence by the committee chairman in a stated intent will very likely be relied upon by the courts in the absence of objection or other reliable evidence of an opposite intent.

The House debate on the recently passed Landrum-Griffin Bill contains an excellent example of the use of this device. When this bill came to the House floor originally it contained a provision which in effect outlawed the use of secondary boycotts in labor disputes. As the section was written, it would probably have been interpreted as extending the secondary boycott prohibition to economic pressure used against non-union employers in the ladies' garment industry which operate under a jobber-contractor system of production. Congressman Teller, of New York, was most anxious to prevent such an interpretation and toward this end entered into a colloquy with both Congressman Griffin and Congressman Landrum. In answer to questions, both gentlemen assured Mr. Teller that the bill would not have the feared effect.[1] In 1949 a similar colloquy on this same subject took place between Senator Ives and Senator Taft during consideration of the Taft-Hartley Act.[2] There is no doubt but that these explanations in both instances could be used as evidence of congressional intent.

In earlier cases the courts completely refused to consider legislative debates in determining congressional intent. Chief Justice Taney, in an 1845 opinion on the construction of the Compromise Tariff Act of 1833, *Aldridge v. Williams*, 44 U.S. (3 How.) 9, 24 (1845) said:

> In expounding this law the judgment of the court cannot, in any degree, be influenced by the construction placed upon it by individual members of Congress in the debate which took place on its passage, nor by the motives or reasons assigned by them for supporting or opposing amendments that were offered. The law as it passed is the will of the majority of both houses, and the only mode in which that will is spoken is in the act itself; and we must gather their intention from the language there used, comparing it, when any ambiguity exists, with the laws upon the same subject, and looking, if necessary, to the public history of the times in which it was passed.

---

1. CONG. RECORD, page 14508, 86th Cong. 1st Sess.

2. CONG. RECORD, page 8709, Part 7, Vol. 95, 81st Cong. 1st Sess.

This view was reiterated in *United States v. Union Pacific R. R. Co.*, 91 U.S. 72, 79 (1875), in which the Court held that the railway company was not obligated to pay interest prior to maturity on bonds issued by the United States under statutes enacted in 1862 and amended in 1864. In reaching this conclusion, the Court said:

> In construing an Act of Congress, we are not at liberty to recur to the views of individual members in debate, nor to consider the motives which influenced them to vote for or against its passage. The Act itself speaks the will of Congress, and this is to be ascertained from the language used . . .

Gradually this strict interpretation gave way to more flexibility, and after 1890, some opinions considered committee reports to resolve ambiguities. There is still great reluctance, however, to give weight to debates on the floor. This is evidenced by the Supreme Court opinion in *United States v. Trans-Missouri Freight Association*, 166 U.S. 290, 316, 318–9 (1897), in which Justice Peckham discusses the effect of congressional debates upon the interpretation of statutes:

> It is also urged that the debates in Congress show beyond a doubt that the act as passed does not include railroads . . .

> There is . . . a general acquiescence in the doctrine that debates in Congress are not appropriate sources of information from which to discover the meaning of the language of a statute passed by that body. [Cases cited *supra*.]

> The reason is that it is impossible to determine with certainty what construction was put upon an act by the members of a legislative body that passed it by resorting to the speeches of individual members thereof. Those who did not speak may not have agreed with those who did; and those who spoke might differ from each other; the result being that the only proper way to construe a legislative act is from the language used in the act, and, upon occasion, by a resort to the history of the times when it was passed . . .

Necessarily, however, courts have come to give consideration to statements of particular Senators and Congressmen who are in charge of the bills, and also to colloquies and other material outside the language of the statute where doubt exists and construction is permissible.

Some extremely important decisions have turned directly on legislative debate involving a planned colloquy. A good example of such a decision was *Duplex Printing Co. v. Deering*, 254 U.S. 443, 475 (1921). This case involved a boycott in New York by a machinists union to compel a manufacturer to unionize its factory in Michigan. The Court of Appeals for the Second Circuit held that the Clayton Act forbade an injunction because it legalized "secondary boycotts". That decision was reversed by the Supreme Court on the ground that the legislative history of the Clayton Act showed that it was not the intention to legalize the "secondary boycott." The Court referred directly to the following colloquy which took place on the floor of the House between Congressman Webb, the manager of the bill, and Congressman Volstead: [3]

Mr. Volstead. Would not this [Section 20 of the Clayton Act] also legalize the secondary boycott? . . .

Mr. Webb. Mr. Chairman, I do not think it legalizes a secondary boycott.

* * *

Mr. Volstead. . . . Can there be any doubt this is intended, or does, in fact, legalize the secondary boycott?

Mr. Webb. I will say frankly to my friend when this section was drawn it was drawn with the careful purpose not to legalize the secondary boycott, and we do not think it does. There may be a difference of opinion about it, but it is the opinion of the committee that it does not legalize the secondary boycott and is not intended to do so.

* * *

Mr. Webb. . . . I should vote for the amendment offered by the gentleman from Minnesota [Mr. Volstead] if I were not perfectly satisfied that it is taken care of in this section. The language the gentleman reads does not authorize the secondary boycott, and he could not torture it into any such meaning. While it does authorize persons to cease to patronize the party

---

3. CONG. RECORD, pages 9652–9658, Vol. 51, Part 10, 63d Cong.2d Sess.

to the dispute, and to recommend to others to cease to patronize that same party to the dispute, that is not a secondary boycott, and you cannot possibly make it mean a secondary boycott . . .

Nevertheless the Court of Appeals made it mean a secondary boycott, and it is quite possible that the Supreme Court could have interpreted it the same way had it not been for the above colloquy. The opinion of the Supreme Court includes the following:

> The majority of the circuit court of appeals, very properly treating the case as involving a secondary boycott, based the decision upon the view that it was the purpose of Sec. 20 to legalize the secondary boycott, "at least in so far as it rests on or consists of refusing to work for any one who deals with the principal offender." Characterizing the section as "blindly drawn," and conceding that the meaning attributed to it was broad, the court referred to the legislative history of the enactment as a warrant for the construction adopted. Let us consider this.
>
> By repeated decisions of this court it has come to be well established that the debates in Congress expressive of the views and motives of individual members are not a safe guide, and hence may not be resorted to, in ascertaining the meaning and purpose of the law-making body . . . But reports of committees of House or Senate stand upon a more solid footing, and may be regarded as an exposition of the legislative intent in a case where otherwise the meaning of a statute is obscure . . . *And this has been extended to include explanatory statements in the nature of a supplemental report made by the committee member in charge of a bill in course of passage* . . . (Italics added.)
>
> In the case of the Clayton Act, the printed committee reports are not explicit with respect to the meaning of the "ceasing to patronize" clause of what is now Sec. 20 . . . the report was supplemented in this regard by the spokesman of the House committee (Mr. Webb), who had the bill in charge when it was under consideration by the House.

Another such colloquy, also in the field of labor legislation, had a direct effect on a later decision by the National

Labor Relations Board. During a debate on the Senate floor in 1949, Senator Pepper closely questioned Senator Taft regarding the effect of a provision broadening the jurisdiction of the NLRB which was contained in the Taft-Hartley Act. Senator Taft replied in positive language that under the Taft-Hartley law it was not the intention to broaden NLRB jurisdiction under the circumstances described by Senator Pepper. In *Hotel Employees Local No. 255 v. Leedom*, 147 F.Supp. 308–9 (1957), affirmed 249 F.2d 506 (1957), the District Court, in affirming the refusal of the NLRB to take jurisdiction, quoted the following statement of Senator Robert A. Taft on the floor of the Senate on August 30, 1949:

> . . . The Taft-Hartley law did not change in any way the language providing for the jurisdiction of the Board, or the general definition of interstate commerce . . . It was not my intention in 1947, nor do I believe it was the intention of other members of the Committee on Labor and Public Welfare, to broaden or extend the jurisdiction of the Board in that respect. In fact, I feel very strongly that it should not be done . . . A hotel performs its service within four walls. It ships nothing into commerce. It produces no goods for commerce. In my opinion the Act was never intended to cover the hotel industry. [Quoted from St. Louis Hotel Association case, supra, at page 1390, citing *Congressional Record*, 81st Congress, First Session, pages 12,697 and 12,698.]

It is significant to note that this last colloquy occurred two years after the Taft-Hartley Act had been passed in 1947. Despite this, the comments of the author of the bill in the Senate had the effect of determining congressional intent.

One of the most recent colloquies that may bear upon the interpretation of a statute was that involving advances to the Highway Trust Fund during the fiscal year ending June 30, 1960. This colloquy took place on September 12, 1959, and in it Senator Holland, who was Chairman of the Appropriations Subcommittee on the Highway Bill, described his understanding that advances made from the general fund of the Treasury to the Highway Trust Fund would be repaid.

There is every reason to believe that we will have a continuing emphasis on such expressions of legislators during debate on the floors of Congress.

4. OVERUSE

Apart from problems of availability, reliability, and manipulation, critics charge that legislative history is being overused by advocates and by courts. They are too quick to resort to the "ashcans" of the legislative process and tend to over-interpret what they find. Suppose, for example, that while a bill for a statute is being debated in the legislature, an amendment is considered and *rejected* by the legislature. What conclusions should be drawn on the basis of this rejection? That the legislature did not intend to include the provisions of the amendment in the statute that was enacted? Or, that the amendment was superfluous because the legislature thought that the provisions of the amendment were already included in the original bill? It is arguably self-deceptive to assume that legislative history will automatically yield clarity in the search for meaning.

Another complaint of the critics is that the users of legislative history fail to understand that the documents of this history do not constitute law:

> It is not to be supposed that, in signing a bill the President endorses the whole Congressional Record. Schwegmann Brothers v. Calvert Distillers Corp., 341 U.S. 384, 396, 71 S.Ct. 745, 751, 95 L.Ed. 1035 (1951) (Justice Jackson concurring).

The goal of these critics is to limit the use of legislative history to those circumstances where the language of the statute is ambiguous. If this is not done, there is a danger that legislative history will be used to alter the intent of the legislature as clearly expressed in the language of the statute. In short, the concern is that the legislative history will be substituted for the statute itself. The entire process is turned on its head, as reflected in the standard joke that a court will examine the language of a statute only if the legislative history of the statute is ambiguous! J. Cory, *The Use of*

Legislative History in the Interpretation of Statutes, 32 Can.Bar Rev. 624, 636 (1954).

The problem, however, is that advocates frequently disagree over whether the language of a statute is ambiguous. The plain meaning rule (p. 75) applies only when there is plain meaning. Law offices spend vast amounts of time and resources trying to demonstrate that statutes are ambiguous. Generally they have been very successful. It is not surprising, therefore, that the use of legislative history is increasing as courts struggle to interpret and apply statutes to concrete facts before them. The criticism of legislative history has had almost no effect on this increase. As indicated earlier, an advocate who does not appear with an argument based on legislative history is usually considered unprepared.

Assignment # 36

Mary Franklin is a registered practitioner before the U.S. Patent Office. She is a nonlawyer who has been registered by and authorized to practice before the Patent Office. She has an office in the state where she meets her clients, renders opinions on patentability, and prepares legal instruments such as applications for letters patent. The state bar association claims that she is illegally practicing law and is seeking an injunction to stop her unless she becomes a member of the bar. In 15 U.S.C. § 31 Congress has provided that the Commissioner of Patents:

> may prescribe regulations governing the conduct of agents, attorneys, or other persons representing applicants or other parties before the Patent Office.

The commissioner has established procedures for the registration of lawyers and nonlawyers to practice before it. The state bar association, however, claims that these procedures are invalid insofar as they authorize practice by nonlawyers, since Congress did not intend such authorization in § 31. Mary (and the Patent Office) disagree with this interpretation of § 31.

a. What is Mary's argument based on the language of § 31? What is the bar's argument? Is this language ambiguous? Is there a need to resort to the legislative history of § 31?

b. When § 31 was first introduced in Congress, it read that the commissioner "may prescribe regulations governing the recognition and conduct of agents, attorneys, or other persons representing applicants or other parties before the Patent Office." This language, however, was amended. The version passed by Congress contained the language quoted on page 119. What arguments can be made on the interpretation of § 31 based on this data of legislative history?

c. On the floor of the Senate during debate on this provision, the following exchange occurred between Senator Davis and Senator Kline:

> Senator DAVIS: I would like to ask the distinguished Senator if this bill would allow the Commissioner of Patents to set a maximum limit on the amount of fees that a lawyer can charge clients for services rendered in connection with a case before the Patent Office?

> Senator KLINE: We examined that question carefully in committee, Senator, and it was our view that any conduct of representatives can be regulated by the Commissioner including the question of fees. I should point out, however, that we did not find much problem with the way in which the bar associations currently handle the question of excessive fees.

What arguments can be made on the interpretation of § 31 based on this data of legislative history?

d. In the report of the Senate committee that recommended the adoption of this law, the following comment is made: "This provision is not intended to authorize persons not members of the bar to practice law." What arguments can be made on the interpretation of § 31 based on this data of legislative history?

Section D. Research of Legislative History

1. FEDERAL STATUTES

When researching the legislative history of a statute, the first question you should ask yourself is whether someone has already compiled its legislative history. A government agency or a private organization may have collected the documents in one set of volumes. Find out where the nearest federal depository library is in your area. These libraries receive numerous documents relevant to federal statutes. Ask whether they have any compilations of legislative histories. This same question should be asked of any other law library to which you have access. You also might inquire whether the local association of law librarians has prepared a list of law libraries that have compiled the legislative histories of certain federal statutes. (In some areas this list is called the *Union List of Legislative Histories*.) If the statute involves a certain federal administrative agency which has an office near you, contact the law division of the agency to determine whether it has a compilation of the legislative history which you can use. If you cannot locate a compilation, you will have to piece together the components of the legislative history on your own.

Most of the federal statutes you will be researching will have a Public Law number assigned to it once it is enacted. (PL 89–285 is the 285th public law enacted by the 89th Congress.) You can obtain the PL number of a statute by examining the end of a particular section of the statute as it is printed in any one of the following three sets of books: *United States Code, United States Code Annotated, or United States Code Service.* The PL number can also be found in *Statutes at Large*, which is where the statute is printed before it goes into these three sets. Some of these statutes also have popular names, e.g., the Civil Rights Act of 1964. When researching the legislative history of a federal statute, it is helpful to know its PL number and its popular name, if any. The history often can be traced through one or both of these identifications.

The following sets of books and materials may be helpful in your search:

(a) U.S. Code Congressional & Administrative News This set of books contains many committee reports. In recent years the set has also printed all of the statutes at large. It is published by West Publishing Company.

(b) Congressional Record This is a daily publication of what takes place in Congress. It contains copies of bills, amendments, transcripts of debates on the floor of the House and Senate, etc. Some of the index features of this set of books include: Daily Digest, History of Bills Enacted into Public Law, Index, etc. The U.S. Government Printing Office publishes the Congressional Record.

(c) Congressional Information Service Index This set of books indexes and abstracts the documents of legislative history for statutes enacted after 1970, e.g., hearings, committee reports. This same material is also provided on microfiche. It is published by Congressional Information Service. See also its Legislative History Service, Annotated Directories.

(d) Digest of Public General Bills This set of books, published by the Library of Congress, contains summaries of bills in Congress. Tables are included on bills that were enacted into law. You also can determine whether committee reports were prepared on the bills.

(e) CCH Congressional Index This is a looseleaf set of books that indexes and digests bills, gives references to hearings, committee reports, etc. It is published by Commerce Clearing House.

(f) Monthly Catalog of U.S. Documents This publication will tell you which committee hearings have been published. It also indexes the reports of the committees.

2. STATE STATUTES

Unlike federal statutes, there is usually no coherent way of researching the legislative history of state statutes. Committee reports often are not published. The testimony at committee hearings may not even be transcribed. Start your search with the legislature itself: the individual committee, if known, that acted on the bill; the office of the legislative counsel; the legislative drafting office; the law librarian for the legislature or the state. Also check the office of the attorney general, corporation counsel, or secretary of state. Try to find someone who can provide some guidance on tracing the history of a particular statute. In a few states there are commercial legislative services that give at least skeleton information on legislators that sponsored bills, committees that considered them, dates of amendments, etc. If there is a Law Revision Commission in your state, check to see whether it has collected any of the documents of legislative history or can provide you with leads. Finally, determine whether there is anything comparable to the Congressional Record at the state level which chronicles the daily activities of the legislature, e.g., a regularly published journal of proceedings or a register.

Chapter Eight

Strict Construction

Section A.   Introduction

Occasionally you will find courts distinguishing between strict construction and liberal construction of statutes:

Strict Construction:
A narrow reading of the statutory language; when there is doubt about whether the language should be interpreted broadly or narrowly, the latter is preferred; when there is doubt as to whether the language is more inclusive or less inclusive, the latter is preferred.

Liberal Construction:
A broad reading of the statutory language; when there is doubt about whether the language should be interpreted broadly or narrowly, the former is preferred; when there is doubt as to whether the language is more inclusive or less inclusive, the former is preferred.

Certain kinds of statutes, as we shall see, call for a strict construction, while others are usually given a liberal construction. This does not mean that the choice between strict and liberal is made in spite of what the legislature intended. Quite the contrary. One or the other is used, *because* it is deemed to be in accord with the intent of the legislature and the objective it sought to achieve in passing the statute. In this sense the distinction between strict and liberal construction adds nothing to the basic rules of construction: the plain meaning rule (p. 75), the mischief rule (p. 76), and the golden rule (p. 81). A strict or a liberal construction will be invalid if it goes against the manifest intent of the legislature.

Section B.   Criminal Laws

As a general rule, penal or criminal statutes are strictly construed against the government and in favor of the accused. Phrased another way, the statute is strictly construed against the side seeking its enforcement and in favor of the side against whom the criminal proceeding is brought.

Obviously it is a drastic step for a criminal prosecution to be brought against someone. If there is doubt as to the meaning of a criminal statute, the doubt should be resolved in favor of the accused. Citizens must have fair notice of the conduct that might subject them to prosecution. Such notice arguably does not exist if a criminal statute is vague and susceptible to more than one interpretation. (Indeed, constitutional challenges might be successfully brought against such statutes.) To remove the potential unfairness, the court will presume that the legislature intended the *least* inclusive definition of the statutory language that is in doubt.

But the doubt must be real. If the intent of the legislature is clearly to criminalize certain conduct, an accused is not home free simply by showing that it is *possible* to interpret language in the statute more than one way. The question is whether the boundary line of prohibited conduct in the statute can be clearly understood by ordinary citizens as opposed to being a trap for the unwary because of loose language in the statute. *If the statute is clear, there is no need to construe it strictly:*

> That criminal statutes are to be strictly construed is a proposition which calls for the citation of no authority. But this does not mean that every criminal statute must be given the narrowest possible meaning in complete disregard of the purpose of the legislature. United States v. Bramblett, 348 U.S. 503, 509–10, 75 S.Ct. 504, 508, 99 L.Ed. 594 (1955).

The problem, of course, arises when such legislative "purpose" is *not* clear. In such cases the accused will be given the benefit of the doubt, as he was in the following famous case.

In McBoyle v. United States, 283 U.S. 25, 51 S.Ct. 340, 75 L.Ed. 816 (1931), the defendant was convicted of transporting an airplane from Illinois to Oklahoma in violation of § 408. He knew the plane was stolen.

> § 408. That whoever shall transport or cause to be transported in interstate or foreign commerce a motor vehicle, knowing the same to have been stolen, shall be punished by a fine of not more than $5,000, or by imprisonment of not more than five years, or both. . . . The term "motor vehicle" shall include an automobile, automobile truck, automobile wagon, motor cycle, or any other self-propelled vehicle not designed for running on rails.

The question was whether an airplane was a "motor vehicle". Justice Holmes held that it was not. "No doubt etymologically it is possible to use the word to signify a conveyance working on land, water or air, . . . [b]ut in everyday speech 'vehicle' calls up the picture of a thing moving on land." 283 U.S. at 26, 51 S.Ct. at 340. If the definition of "motor vehicle" is taken literally, an airplane is a "vehicle not designed for running on rails." But this is not the meaning that an ordinary citizen would use. Hence the Court strictly construed the statute in favor of the accused.

When an ambiguous *criminal* statute is before the courts, they should not enlarge the scope of the statute by speculating about whether the legislature would have included a certain term if it had thought about it:

> Although it is not likely that a criminal will carefully consider the text of the law before he murders or steals, it is reasonable that a fair warning should be given to the world in language that the common world will understand, of what the law intends to do if a certain line is passed. To make the warning fair, so far as possible the line should be clear. When a rule of conduct is laid down in words that evoke in the common mind only the picture of vehicles moving on land, the statute should not be extended to aircraft simply because it may seem to us that a similar policy applies, or upon the speculation that if the legislature had thought of it, very likely broader words would have been used. 283 U.S. at 27, 51 S.Ct. at 341.

Assignment # 37

Reread the statute involved in the Caminetti case, p. 1. Would this statute be violated by a minister who took his three wives across the state line? (Assume he practiced polygamy as a dictate of his religion.)

Assignment # 38

Section 77 makes it a crime "to stand in the street obstructing traffic." Helen is obstructing traffic as she walks across the street. She did not wait until the light was in her favor. Has she violated § 77?

Assignment # 39

James Turley borrowed a friend's car in South Carolina, telling the friend that he wanted to drive several people to locations within this state. Instead, he took the car to Maryland, where he sold it and used the proceeds for his own use. Has Turley violated § 2312?

Statute: § 2312. Whoever transports in interstate or foreign commerce a motor vehicle or aircraft, knowing the same to have been stolen, shall be fined not more than $5,000 or imprisoned not more than five years, or both.

Assignment # 40

Draft a statute on any topic in which you make certain conduct a crime. The instructor will select some of the students to read their statutes out loud in class, or to write them on the blackboard or on a flip chart. The job of the rest of the class is to think of fact situations that do not appear to fall within the letter of the statute, but are debatable. The class then discusses whether the statute applies to each fact situation and whether the rule of strict construction is appropriate.

Section C. Statutes in Derogation of the Common Law

As we have seen, the common law is judge-made law in the absence of controlling statutory law (p. 6). The legislature can always pass a statute changing the common law. Such statutes are said to be in *derogation* of the common law. In our early legal history, courts looked with disfavor upon statutes in derogation of the common law. In part this was due to a sense of judicial superiority and a distrust of the legislature. As a consequence, courts strictly construed statutes in derogation of the common law. The statutes were interpreted narrowly so as to lead to the least possible change of the common law. Today this distrust is much less prevalent. Yet the doctrine of strict construction still exists, although with more limited force.

By nature, much of the common law at least appears to be unstructured. (It has been affectionately referred to as a "seemless web.") It grows and develops in piecemeal fashion on a case-by-case basis. Hence, when the legislature decides to change some of the common law, it is sometimes unclear exactly how much is being changed. The legislature can easily change a statute by simply repealing a certain section number of the code. It can be much more difficult to pinpoint a change in the common law since the latter is a composite of tradition reflected in thousands of prior court opinions. This can create doubt in interpreting a statute in derogation of the common law. Precisely what common law did the legislature intend to change? The occasional difficulty of answering this question, plus whatever jealousy that courts still retain over the realm of the common law, accounts for the inclination of a court to strictly construe statutes in derogation of the common law. When in doubt, a court will tend to preserve as much of the common law as possible in the face of a statute that is less than articulate in chipping away some of it.

At common law, for example, a married woman could not sue anyone in her own name for personal injuries against her. Her husband had to join in the suit. Assume that the legislature passes a statute giving her the right to bring such suits in her own name. A court might strictly construe this change in the common law by holding that she still could not bring the suit if her *husband* is the one who allegedly injured her. The statute would be narrowly interpreted to cover suits against third parties and hence preserve that portion of the common law which provided that a wife could not sue her husband for personal injuries.

The rule of strict construction will not apply if it is clear what portion of the common law the legislature intends to change. "The rule that statutes in derogation of the common law are to be strictly construed does not require" a court to "defeat an obvious legislative purpose." Jamison v. Encarnacion, 281 U.S. 635, 640, 50 S.Ct. 440, 442, 74 L.Ed. 1082 (1930).

Section D. Remedial Legislation

[A] remedial statute must be liberally construed, so as to effectuate its object and purposes. Although due regard will be given to the language used, such [a statute] will be construed, when its meaning is doubtful, so as to suppress the mischief at which it is directed, and to advance or extend the remedy provided, and bring within the scope of the law every case which comes clearly within its spirit and policy. Lande v. Jurisich, 59 Cal.App.2d 613, 139 P.2d 657, 659 (Cal.Dist.Ct.App.1943)

The definition of a remedial statute is quite broad. It is any statute that creates a remedy or improves a remedy already existing for the enforcement of rights and the redress of injuries; it is a statute that corrects defects, mistakes, or omissions in the law. J. Sutherland, *Statutes and Statutory Interpretation*, § 60.02 (4th ed., D. Sands, 1973). Under such a broad definition, few noncriminal statutes would *not* be classified as remedial. Hence the rule that remedial legislation is to be liberally construed is little more than a statement of the mischief rule (p. 76). Criminal statutes as well as statutes that impose severe penalties are strictly construed; everything else is broadly construed, unless otherwise indicated, to effectuate the legislative purpose in the statute.

Chapter Nine

Mandatory Language

When examining a law, one of your first concerns should be to distinguish between what is required (mandatory) and what is a matter of choice (discretionary). The former is usually indicated by words such as "shall" or "must", and the latter by words such as "may". These words are either expressed or implied in the language used. As part of your initial reading and assessment of the law, it is a good idea to categorize the language into what appears to be mandatory, discretionary, and doubtful (see Figure 4).

Mandatory Components of Section 304.03(a)

1. Each registrant *shall* maintain the records and inventories.

2. Each registrant *shall* file the reports required.

3. Any registrant authorized to conduct designated activities (pursuant to sections 301.22(b) or 307.11–307.15) *shall* maintain records and inventories and *shall* file the required reports.

4. When a researcher manufactures a controlled item, he *must* keep a record of the quantity manufactured.

Figure 4. Mandatory and Discretionary Language

DISCRETIONARY: MANDATORY:

§ 304.03 Persons required to keep records and file reports.

(a) Each registrant shall maintain the records ◄——— 1
and inventories and shall file the reports required ◄——— 2
by this part, except as exempted by this section.
Any registrant who is authorized to conduct other
activities without being registered to conduct
those activities, either pursuant to § 301.22(b) of
this chapter or pursuant to §§ 307.11–307.15 of
this chapter, shall maintain the records and inventories and shall file the reports required by this ◄——— 3
part for persons registered to conduct such activi-

a ——► ties. This latter requirement should not be construed as requiring stocks of controlled substances
being used in various activities under one registration to be stored separately, nor that separate

b ——► records are required for each activity. The intent
of the Bureau is to permit the registrant to keep
one set of records which are adapted by the registrant to account for controlled substances used in

c ——► any activity. Also, the Bureau does not wish to
acquire separate stocks of the same substance to
be purchased and stored for separate activities.
Otherwise, there is no advantage gained by per-
mitting several activities under one registration.
Thus, when a researcher manufactures a controlled
item, he must keep a record of the quantity manu- ◄——— 4
factured; when he distributes a quantity of the
item, he must use and keep invoices or order ◄——— 5
forms to document the transfer; when he imports
a substance, he keeps as part of his records the ◄——— 6
documentation required of an importer; and when

d ——► substances are used in chemical analysis, he need
not keep a record of this because such a record
would not be required of him under a registration

e ——► to do chemical analysis. All of these records may
be maintained in one consolidated record system.

f ——► Similarly, the researcher may store all of his controlled items in one place, and every two years
take inventory of all items on hand, regardless of
whether the substances were manufactured by
him, imported by him, or purchased domestically
by him, or whether the substances will be administered to subjects, distributed to other researchers,
or destroyed during chemical analysis.

5. When such a researcher distributes a quantity of such items, he *must* use and keep documentation of the transfer.

6. When a researcher imports a substance, does he *have* to keep the documentation records required of an importer? The preceding clauses explicitly used the word "must", but the word is absent in this clause on importing. Is the word implied? Would the word be superfluous because the documentation is already required of an importer? The documentation may be mandatory as import records, but are they required for purposes of § 304.03? Are two separate sets of records being referred to? Researcher records and importer records? Documentation is required only as to the latter?

Discretionary Components of 304.03(a)

a. Stocks of controlled substances being used in various activities under one registration *could* be stored separately, but they do not have to be.

b. As to each activity, separate records *could* be maintained for each such activity, but they do not have to be.

c. We are told what the Bureau does not "wish" to do. It does not wish to acquire separate stocks of the same substance to be purchased and stored for separate activities. But *could* it acquire such separate stocks? Is it required *not* to do so?

d. When substances are used in chemical analysis by a researcher, he *could* keep a record of this, but he *need not* do so.

e. All of the records *may* be maintained in one consolidated record system, but they do not have to be.

f. A researcher *may* store all controlled items in one place and take inventory every two years of all items on hand, but he *need not* do it this way.

Again, it must be stressed that the above analysis is only preliminary. The assessment is based solely on an initial reaction to the language. Our objective is limited at this point: to identify *possible* interpretations, including areas of potential ambiguity and doubt. From this point we must then move to all of the other aids of interpretation, e.g., the mischief rule, the golden rule, other canons of construction, legislative history. We must use these aids to challenge our surface reading. It may be that the legislature intended the word "shall" to be permissive rather than mandatory in some of the clauses. Similarly, the word "may" could fall into either category.

> Although generally the word "shall" in the statute is used in the mandatory sense, it is true that "shall" may be construed as permissive where from the circumstances it is obvious that the Legislature intended it so. .   .   .   Prince v. Hunter, 388 So.2d 546, 548 (Ala.1980).

> The courts   .   .   . have interpreted "may" to be both permissive and mandatory. When the exact meaning cannot be determined from the language used in the statute, the courts in the search to ascertain the legislative intent look to the words, context, subject matter, effects and consequences as well as to the spirit and purpose of the statute. Apache East, Inc. v. Wiegand, 119 Ariz. 308, 580 P.2d 769, 773 (App.1978)

A distinction is sometimes made between mandatory provisions and *directory* provisions in a statute. Mandatory provisions go to the essence of the statute. They must be complied with in order to obtain the advantages or other consequences of the statute. Directory provisions, on the other hand, are instructions or directions that are primarily matters of convenience. This is not to say that directory provisions can be disobeyed or ignored. Noncompliance, however, will not necessarily be fatal. Directory provisions might be phrased in "shall" or "must" language, but this will not be controlling. As always, the question is what the legislature intended:

> Whether a statute is mandatory or directory does not depend upon its form, but upon the intention of the legislature, to be ascertained from a consideration of the entire act, its nature, its object, and the consequences that would result from construing it one way or the other. In re McQuiston's Adoption, 238 Pa. 304, 86 A. 205, 206 (1913).

If a provision is directory, then it often will be treated as a matter of discretion, or simply as something which is not essential to the operation of the statute.

Assume that the following statute governs candidates for elective office:

§ 47. To qualify for placement on the ballot, a candidate must file the requisite number of signatures specified in § 43(b) at the County Election Commission's office at least thirty days before the next scheduled election. A failure to do so shall result in the candidate's name not being printed on the ballot.

An individual gathers the correct number of signatures and tries to file them at the office of the County Election Commission 31 days before the next scheduled election. They cannot be filed, however, because of a fire at the Commission office; there is no one to file them with. Can this individual's name be printed on the ballot? The statute uses mandatory language: "must" and "shall". But is the time requirement merely directory in such a case? Is time always of the essence? Arguably, the legislature did not intend a disqualification here. It is reasonable to read an exception into the statute. Disqualification was not intended if the individual did not file on time through no fault of his or her own. The Commission impliedly is given discretion to waive the time requirement in such unusual circumstances. This interpretation would most effectively carry out the purpose of the legislature (mischief rule). The legislature could not have intended the harsh consequence of disqualification in such a case; it would make no sense (golden rule).

Assignment # 41

Statute: § 909. A forced sale of a home shall be ordered due to delinquent real estate taxes unless there is enough personal property within the home of sufficient value to cover the amount of the delinquent taxes.

Facts: Smith owns a home on Vine Street. Delinquent taxes on the home amount to $1,580. The value of Smith's furniture in the home is $300. There is also a stereo set in the home belonging to Jones, a friend of Smith who is away on vacation. When Jones returns in two months, he will take the stereo set back. It is worth $3,000.

Can a forced sale of Smith's home take place because of the delinquent taxes?

Assignment # 42

Statute: § 41. Defendants accused of crime detained in the County Jail may be allowed one free telephone call per week.

Facts: Dwyer is in the County Jail on a charge of burglary. He requests the free use of the phone during the first week of his incarceration. The warden denies the request. In the second week, the same request is denied again.

Has the warden violated § 41?

Chapter Ten

Grammar and Statutory Interpretation

"Woman, without her, man would be a savage."

"Woman, without her man, would be a savage." [1]

"The teacher says the inspector is a fool."

"The teacher, says the inspector, is a fool." [2]

Statutes are written in the English language. Communication occurs through a particular combination of words. The grammatical structure of these words helps to convey the intended meaning. Unfortunately, sloppy legislative drafting can make this meaning difficult to identify. The problem of modifiers can be particularly troublesome.

§ 34. This chapter does not apply to executed documents and instruments which evidence a right to the payment of money.

---

1. Brossard, *Punctuation in Statutes*, 24 Oregon Law Rev. 157 (1945). See also Nutting, *The Perils of Punctuation*, 53 American Bar Association Journal 1072 (1967).

2. Driedger, *Legislative Drafting*, 27 Canadian Bar Review 291 (1949).

What does "executed" modify?

• Only "documents"?

• Either "documents" or "instruments"? (Does "and" mean "or"?)

What does the "which" clause modify?

• Only "instruments"?

• Either "instruments" or "documents"? (Does "and" mean "or"?)

> § 7. Acceptable evidence includes evidence in writing or oral testimony unless the Commissioner determines that time would be wasted thereby.

What does the "unless" clause modify?

• Only "oral testimony"?

• Either "oral testimony" or "evidence in writing"?

Can the commissioner refuse to accept *written* evidence deemed to be a waste of time? Only if the second option above is the correct interpretation.

Assignment # 43

Apply § 83 to the facts.

Statute: § 83. All radio stations need not run any programs geared to the senior citizen audience nor to the children's audience if written permission not to conduct such programming is obtained from the Commission. Station managers, but not announcers, must obtain a 1032 clearance license. No hours of broadcasting, except between 12 midnight and 6 a.m., may contain programming on a subject matter dealing with sex unless the sexual references consist of quotes from medical doctors or the programming is documentary in character where a copy of the transcript of the program is mailed to the Commission within five days of its airing.

Facts: WEZE is a small, local radio station. It has been charged with violating § 83. The only staff member of the station is Barry King, who is the station manager, the public relations officer, the announcer, and the secretary. He is charged with failing to seek a 1032 clearance license; with airing a documentary dealing with sex at 4 p.m. (a twenty-minute interview by King with a prostitute in which the latter described hospital treatment for venereal disease) and not submitting a transcript of the program to the Commission; and finally with failing to conduct any programs geared to senior citizens without the written permission of the Commission not to air such programs.

It is sometimes said that the punctuation of a statute is not part of the law. This, however, is overstated. It is more accurate to say that courts will not allow punctuation to overcome the natural meaning of the words used and the manifest intent of the legislature. Courts are understandably reluctant to engage in an extended debate over the meaning of commas, semicolons, and periods. To avoid this, there was a time in early English history when the statutes of Parliament were not punctuated at all. Today there is less worry that an analysis of the punctuation of a statute will supplant the analysis of the statute's substance. In fact, courts often point out how punctuation supports a particular interpretation.

A good example is United States v. Republic Steel Corp., 362 U.S. 482, 80 S.Ct. 884, 4 L.Ed.2d 903 (1960). The defendant deposited a large quantity of industrial waste in a river. Although the waste was in the form of small particles, it eventually collected and settled in the bottom of the river. This resulted in a substantial decrease in the depth of the river. The defendant was charged with violating § 10 of the Rivers and Harbors Act:

> That the creation of any obstruction not affirmatively author-ized by Congress, to the navigable capacity of any of the waters of the United States is hereby prohibited; and it shall not be lawful to build or commence the building of any wharf, pier, dolphin, boom, weir, breakwater, bulkhead, jetty, or other structures . . . . [unless] authorized by the Secretary of the Army.

The question was whether the waste deposits constituted an "obstruction" under § 10. The defendant argued that an "obstruction" must be a "structure" of a kind similar to a wharf, pier, etc. The collected particle waste was not such a structure.

The court rejected this interpretation, relying in part on the grammar of § 10. Note that a semicolon separates the two main parts of § 10. The first part refers to an "obstruction", while the second part mentions "structures". A semicolon can be a substitute for a period. Clauses separated by a semicolon are related, but they could stand alone. The clauses separated by this punctuation often contain thoughts that are independent, although related. The semicolon suggests that Congress was not talking about obstructions that *are* structures. Rather, it was prohibiting obstructions *and* structures.

> It is argued that "obstruction" means some kind of structure. The design of § 10 should be enough to refute that argument, since the ban of "any obstruction," unless approved by Congress, appears in the first part of § 10, followed by a semicolon and another provision which bans various kinds of structures unless authorized by the Secretary of the Army. 362 U.S. at 486, 80 S.Ct. at 887.

Chapter Eleven

Retroactive/Prospective Operation of Statutes

On March 13, 1966, the legislature passes the following statute:

> § 444. Contributory negligence shall not be an absolute bar to recovery by the plaintiff. The jury shall apportion the recovery based on the comparative negligence of the parties.

Prior to the enactment of this statute, if the *plaintiff's* negligence contributed in any way to his or her own injury, there could be no recovery no matter how negligent the defendant was. Contributory negligence was an absolute bar.

The legislature will usually indicate the date on which a new statute such as this will become effective, e.g., in seven days, on January 1, immediately. If no explicit effective date is mentioned and none is implied, a standard computation often will be used, e.g., the statute becomes effective on the day after it is adopted and signed by the chief executive or 30 days after the close of the current session of the legislature. Hence the date that the statute was passed or enacted (March 13, 1966, in our example above) can be different from the effective date of the statute. For purposes of discussion, we will assume the effective date of § 444 is March 13, 1966, that is, it became effective immediately.

Once we know the effective date of a statute, the next problem is to determine whether the statute:

• operates only on events that occur *after* the effective date (prospective operation) *or*

• operates on events that occur *before* the effective date (retroactive operation) as well as on future events

If § 444 is prospective, then the new rule of comparative negligence will apply to negligence actions that arise on or after March 13, 1966, its effective date. The old rule of contributory negligence would continue to apply to negligence actions that arose prior to March 13, 1966 even if the actual suit was brought after this date. In the following three cases, assume that § 444 is prospective and that the plaintiff's negligence contributed to his or her own injury along with the defendant's negligence:

Case A

Date of accident:	2/12/66
Date of suit:	3/1/66
Governing rule:	Contributory negligence; plaintiff recovers nothing; § 444 does not apply since cause of action arose prior to the effective date

Case B

Date of accident:	2/12/66
Date of suit:	3/20/66
Governing rule:	Contributory negligence; plaintiff recovers nothing; § 444 does not apply since cause of action arose prior to the effective date

Case C

Date of accident:	3/15/66
Date of suit:	3/20/66
Governing rule:	Comparative negligence; the plaintiff can recover that portion of the damages caused by the defendant's negligence; § 444 applies since cause of action arose after the effective date

However, if § 444 is retroactive, then the comparative negligence rule would apply to all three cases above.

A further complication would be pre-effective date events that are still involved in litigation *on* the effective date. In Case A, for example, assume that the trial lasted several weeks and did not reach final judgment before March 13, 1966, the effective date of § 444. If the statute is retroactive, comparative negligence would govern. If it is purely prospective, then the rule would be contributory negligence. A combination, however, is possible. The statute may cover post-effective date events *plus* those pre-effective date events that were still the subject of litigation on the effective date.

How do we determine whether a statute is prospective, retroactive, or a combination? The two standards of assessment are the intent of the legislature and the power of the legislature. What did the legislature intend and did it have the power to do what it intended?

Most statutes are prospective. In fact, retroactivity is disfavored, although there are exceptions, as we shall see. The danger of a retroactive statute is its potential for surprise and unfairness. At the time events are occurring, one set of rules apply. Then a statute is passed imposing a new set of rules on these events. This can lead to some harsh results. Consequently, courts are reluctant to hold that a statute is retroactive unless it is clear that this is what the legislature intended. Even if this intent is clear, however, it will not be controlling if retroactivity conflicts with certain fundamental principles of constitutional law.

The U.S. Constitution provides that government shall not pass any "ex post facto Law." U.S. Const., art. I, §§ 9, 10. An ex post facto law would criminalize conduct that was lawful when performed. For example, in 1979 you carry 50 gallons of gasoline in the back seat of your car. No law exists which prohibited this activity. In 1980 the legislature passes a statute making it a misdemeanor to carry gasoline in a car outside of a tank attached to the car. The legislature intends it to have retroactive effect. This statute is unconstitutional. The legislature cannot penalize someone after the fact when the conduct was legal at the time performed. The scope of the prohibition is as follows:

> 1st. Every law that makes an action done before the passing of the law, and which was innocent when done, criminal, and punishes such action. 2d. Every law that aggravates a crime, or that makes it greater than it was when committed. 3d. Every law that changes the punishment, and inflicts a greater punishment than the law annexed to the crime when committed. 4th. Every law that alters the legal rules of evidence, and receives less, or different, testimony, than the law required at the time of the commission of the offense, in order to convict the offender. All these, and similar laws, are manifestly unjust and oppressive. But I do not consider any law ex post facto, within the prohibition, that mollifies the rigor of the criminal law; but only those that create, or aggravate the crime; or increase the punishment, or change the rules of evidence, for the purpose of conviction. Calder v. Bull, 3 U.S. (3 Dall.) 386, 390, 1 L.Ed. 648 (1798), Justice Chase.

Another constitutional doctrine that limits the power of a state to enact retroactive statutes is the Contract Clause: "No State shall . . . pass any . . . Law impairing the Obligation of Contracts. . . ." U.S. Const. art. I, § 10. A legislature could not, for example, pass a statute in 1983 declaring that any debt incurred in 1982 for the purchase of a video game is null and void. The sellers of video games had sales contracts with their customers. To invalidate any remaining debts of these customers certainly impairs the obligation of repayment that they owed to the sellers.

Legislatures are constantly passing statutes regulating the activities of industries and professions of all kinds, e.g., credit transactions, sales of securities, tax transfers. Inevitably the statutes affect contracts already in existence. The state has a broad "police power" to legislate for the public health, safety, morals, and welfare of its people. If statutes passed pursuant to this power are reasonably related to the vital interests of the people, they will be upheld *even though there is some impairment in the contracts of individuals.* The statutes must be protecting some basic societal interest. If, however, the impairment of existing contracts is substantial, the state must show that the statute is a reasonable and narrow method of protecting the societal interest.

A distinction is often made between (a) substantive or vested contract rights and (b) matters of procedure or remedy. Retroactive statutes affecting the latter are much more likely to be sustained as constitutional. For example:

Substance: A statute retroactively reduces the interest that any consumer must pay on any contract to a maximum of 3%.

Remedy: A statute retroactively reduces the statute of limitations (within which all breach-of-contract actions must be brought) from four years to two years.

The first statute drastically impairs the contract obligations of a potentially vast segment of the population. It is highly unlikely that a court would sustain this statute as a valid exercise of the police power. It does not appear to be reasonably related to the protection of a vital societal interest. Even in a national emergency such as a depression, such a statute would probably go too far. Compare this with a statute that extends the redemption period in connection with a foreclosure sale if the mortgagor can pay a substantial portion of the debt. In severe economic times, this statute would probably be allowed. While it significantly affects obligations under existing contracts, the statute is more narrowly drawn and hence more reasonable. This statute is closer to the second statute in the example above which reduced the statute of limitations. Procedural changes and changes in the remedy or method by which a right is enforced are often applied retroactively without any constitutional problems, particularly if the change is reasonable and does not impose any undue hardships on anyone who relied on the prior law.

Retroactive statutes also are challenged on due process grounds. The Constitution provides that government shall not deprive a person of property "without due process of law". U.S. Const. amend. V, amend. XIV. Assume, for example, that the legislature passes a retroactive law requiring mine operators to pay black-lung benefits to coal miners and that the statute covers miners who had retired before the effective date of the statute. Has the legislature deprived the operators of their property without due process of law? No. The statute will be sustained so long as the court finds the statute to be rationally related to a legitimate government purpose. The state has an interest in seeing to it that the health-care needs of its citizens are provided for. A rational way to achieve this objective is to require mining operators to provide compensation to workers who contracted black-lung disease while they were working to the economic advantage of the operators. Since it is relatively easy to establish a rational relationship between a retroactive statute and a legitimate state interest, constitutional challenges on due process grounds are seldom successful.

Assignment # 44

Statutes: § 68. In a prosecution for rape, corroboration of the alleged victim's evidence is needed as to each element of the offense. (1968)

§ 68(a). Section 68 is hereby repealed. (1972)

Facts: Smith is charged with raping Jones on August 9, 1970. At the trial, the only evidence against Smith is the testimony of Jones. Smith is convicted.

What argument can Smith make on appeal?

Assignment # 45

In August of 1978, Jim is sued for negligence by Bob in a Nevada court. Jim is a resident of California; Bob, of Nevada. Jim was driving through Nevada on his way to California when his car collided with Bob's on a Nevada road. Bob was not able to serve Jim with process in Nevada since Jim had left the state when the suit was commenced. Service was obtained by registered mail pursuant to a Nevada long-arm statute passed on September 1, 1978, which authorized service in this manner. Can Jim object to being sued in Nevada?

Assignment # 46

In February of 1980, Mary receives $1000 in dividends from a corporation in which she owns stock. She feels that she should not have to pay the 3% tax on these dividends imposed by § 2626 of the Emergency Revenue Act of 1980. The legislature began consideration of this tax in January of 1980. It was passed in December of 1980 and applied to "all dividends received during 1980 and 1981." The tax is to go out of existence on January 1, 1982. Does Mary have to pay the tax?

Chapter Twelve

Avoiding Constitutional Issues in the Interpretation of Statutes

When the validity of an act of Congress is drawn in question, and even if a serious doubt of constitutionality is raised, it is a cardinal principle that this Court will first ascertain whether a construction is fairly possible by which the [constitutional] question may be avoided. Ashwander v. Tennessee Valley Authority, 297 U.S. 288, 348, 56 S.Ct. 466, 483–4, 80 L.Ed. 688 (1936), Justice Brandeis concurring.

I cannot subscribe to a wholly emasculated construction of a statute to avoid facing a latent constitutional question, in purported fidelity to the salutory doctrine of avoiding unnecessary resolution of constitutional issues, a principle to which I fully adhere. It is, of course, desirable to salvage by construction legislative enactments whenever there is good reason to believe that Congress did not intend to legislate consequences that are unconstitutional, but it is not permissible, in my judgment, to take a lateral step that robs legislation of all meaning in order to avert the collision between its plainly intended purpose and the commands of the Constitution. Welsh v. United States, 398 U.S. 333, 354, 90 S.Ct. 1792, 1804, 26 L.Ed.2d 308 (1970), Justice Harlan, concurring.

151

Declaring a statute unconstitutional is a very drastic step. The judiciary and the legislature are coequal branches of government. As both Justices Brandeis and Harlan suggest in the above quotes, courts are reluctant to use their power of judicial review to invalidate a statute. Statutes are presumed to be constitutional; the legislature is presumed to have intended that its statutes comply with the constitution. Hence, if it is possible to avoid declaring a statute unconstitutional by adopting a certain interpretation of the statute, the courts will do so. Justice Harlan, however, warns us not to go too far in trying to avoid a confrontation between the statute and the constitution. In some cases there may be no alternative interpretation of the statute that will save it from constitutional infirmity.

Assume that the legislature has passed the following statute:

> § 56. A certified abandoned city building shall be given to any man who is the head of the household earning less than $6,000 a year who intends to use the building for residential purposes only.

Helen Thomas is a single parent with three children whom she raises on her own. She earns $4500 a year. She wants to obtain one of the certified abandoned city buildings to live in with her children. Does she qualify? The answer is whether she fits within the category of a "man" under § 56.

The word "man" is arguably ambiguous. It sometimes refers to humankind, including males and females. Other times it refers to males only.

If it is clear that the legislature intended "man" to mean males only, serious constitutional problems would arise. The statute would probably violate the equal protection clause because it creates an irrational classification based on sex. The canons of construction, legislative history, and any other aid to interpretation would have to be used to assess whether this is what the legislature intended. However, *if the doubt remains*, the courts will adopt an interpretation of the word that avoids the constitutional issue if such an interpretation is available. "Humankind" is a possible interpretation of the word "man". This definition would eliminate the constitutional problem. Hence, the courts will presume that this is what the legislature intended.

But again, the alternative interpretation cannot be a fabrication, or, in the words of Justice Harlan, a "wholly emasculated construction" which "robs" the statute of all meaning. In the rush to avoid declaring a statute unconstitutional, the courts cannot rewrite the statute. Before a court will resolve any doubt in favor of the statute's constitutionality, there must be doubt!

Assignment # 47

The first amendment provides that "Congress shall make no law respecting an establishment of religion. . . . " U.S. Const. Amend. I. One of the ways in which this amendment can be violated is through government preferences for one kind of religion over another.

Assume that Congress has passed the following statute on conscientious objectors:

> § 6(j). Nothing contained in this title shall be construed to require any person to be subject to combatant training and service in the armed forces of the United States who, by reason of religious training and belief, is conscientiously opposed to participation in war in any form. Religious training and belief in this connection means an individual's belief in relation to a Supreme Being involving duties superior to those arising from any human relation, but does not include essentially political, sociological, or philosophical views or a merely personal moral code.

Smith is a pacifist and refuses to register for the draft. He believes that killing in war is wrong, unethical, and immoral. His conscience prevents him from taking part in such an evil practice. Smith was brought up in a religious home, but he has not continued his childhood religious ties. He neither affirms nor denies a belief in God.

a. If Smith is denied conscientious-objector status under § 6(j), what argument can be made that § 6(j) is unconstitutional?

b. What interpretation of § 6(j) might save it from being declared unconstitutional?

c. What research steps would you take to determine whether the interpretation you listed in (b) is viable?

Chapter Thirteen

Statutes and Regulations

Most statutes are carried out by administrative agencies. The agency will often write regulations which, as we have seen, are based on the agency's interpretation of the statutes. The legislature may direct the agency to write regulations that implement the policy of the statute. More or less general guidelines must be provided by the legislature in performing this agency task. Even if no direct authorization to write regulations is contained in the statute, the agency will still have the power to write regulations that explain the statute to itself and to the public.

Courts give considerable weight to interpretations of statutes contained in agency regulations, particularly if the regulations have been coherent and have been in existence over a period of time. But agencies can make mistakes in these interpretations. In their enthusiasm for or their hostility against the statute, they may violate the meaning and purpose of the statute. Hence the courts are available to take corrective action. According to Justice Powell:

> It is a commonplace in our jurisprudence that an administrative agency's consistent, longstanding interpretation of the statute under which it operates is entitled to considerable weight. This deference is a product both of an awareness of the practical expertise which an agency normally develops, and of a willingness to accord some measure of flexibility to such an agency as it encounters new and unforeseen problems over time. But

155

this deference is constrained by our obligation to honor the clear meaning of a statute, as revealed by its language, purpose, and history. On a number of occasions in recent years this Court has found it necessary to reject the [agency's] interpretation of the various [statutes it administers]. International Brotherhood of Teamsters, Chauffeurs, Warehousemen and Helpers of America v. Daniel, 439 U.S. 551, 566, 99 S.Ct. 790, 800, 58 L.Ed.2d 808, n. 20 (1979).

Agency administrators are not always neutral technicians who simply carry out the mandate of the statute as they see it. Consider, for example, the following environment: a liberal, Democratic Congress succeeds in passing extensive social welfare legislation signed into law by a Democratic President or by a middle-of-the-road Republican president; a strongly conservative Republican president is then elected who appoints equally conservative executives to the agencies that must administer the social welfare legislation on the books; these executives write arguably restrictive regulations implementing the legislation; charges are made that the regulations are misinterpreting, and indeed, rewriting, the statutes (e.g., in response to a statute that calls for two vegetables to be given to poor children in school-lunch programs, an agency writes a regulation classifying catsup as one of the two vegetables). Politics thus plays a role in the regulatory rule-making process.

The following case presents a good example of how far an agency can go astray (due to political or other reasons) in interpreting a statute.

Mrs. Mary DOE, Individually, and on behalf of her minor dependent children and in behalf of all others similarly situated, Plaintiff,

v.

Edwin FLOWERS, Commissioner of the West Virginia Department of Welfare, Defendant.

364 F.Supp. 953. (N.D.W.Va.1973).

PER CURIAM:

These two class actions which were consolidated for hearing challenge the validity of Section 56242 of the West

Virginia Department of Welfare Assistance Payments Manual.[1] This regulation requires unmarried mothers of applicants and recipients of Aid to Families with Dependent Children to cooperate with the welfare authorities by identifying
the putative fathers of the children and initiating support or
paternity proceedings against them. The only exceptions to
the requirement that the mother identify the father are in
those cases where (1) the mother is an incompetent, (2) the
father is an unknown rapist, or (3) the child is over three
years of age and there is no evidence of paternity which
could be used in court. Under the regulatory pattern if the
mother identifies the father, she then has thirty days in
which she must obtain the father's notarized consent to support the child or file a bastardy warrant against the putative
father or seek the advice of the prosecuting attorney and institute such action as he may recommend.

   These actions were brought by Mary Doe and Jane Doe
and others, individually, and on behalf of their minor dependent children who are applicants or former recipients of assistance under the AFDC program and who have been denied aid solely because their mothers have refused to take
the action required by Section 56242.

   Plaintiffs attack the regulation as incompatible with the
Social Security Act [of Congress].

   The defendants maintain that their denial of aid to the
plaintiffs is not only authorized but required by the federal
statute which provides that the state implement a program
under which the state agency will undertake "in the case of a

----

1. At the time these actions were instituted Section 67200 of the West
Virginia Department of Welfare Eligibility Manual (the predecessor of
Section 56242) was in effect and the complaints were directed against it.
That regulation provided in relevant part:

   "If the parent is unwilling to cooperate in exploring the possibility of
   support from the absent parent, the service worker will notify the Eligibility Specialist to close the case."

The practical administrative application of Section 67200 was the same
as the present regulation, and since the plaintiffs are now being denied
assistance pursuant to Section 56252, the validity of the current regulation
will be the subject of our disposition.

child born out of wedlock who is receiving aid to families with dependent children to establish the paternity of such child and secure support for him." 42 U.S.C.A. § 602(a)(17) (A)(i). While we concede the obligation placed upon the state, we are of the opinion that the method adopted by it is inappropriate and incompatible with the basic eligibility considerations of the Act. The Congress has imposed only two eligibility requirements; they are "need" and "dependency," and the challenged regulation imposes an additional eligibility requirement which is clearly contrary to the congressional intent underlying the AFDC program.

With few exceptions the courts who have had occasion to consider regulations similar to the one presently before us have concluded that they were incompatible with the Act. One of the first of these was Doe v. Shapiro, 302 F.Supp. 761 (D.C.Conn.1969). In a well reasoned opinion the court in that case held the regulation invalid, stating:

> "Although the state argues with considerable force that the Social Security Act requires it to take affirmative steps to ascertain paternity in the case of illegitimate children receiving AFDC assistance, we do not think that 42 U.S.C.A. § 602(a) (17)(A)(i) was ever intended to allow a state to disqualify an otherwise eligible child on the basis of its mother's refusal to name the father, and we do not think that a close reading of that provision will support the interpretation urged by the state. We hold, therefore, that the challenged regulation is invalid on the ground that it imposes an additional condition of eligibility not required by the Social Security Act."

Subsequent to the filing of these actions, the decisions of three courts who had adopted the *Shapiro* rationale have been affirmed per curiam by the Supreme Court. . . .

In the light of these authorities, we hold that Section 56242 of the West Virginia Department of Welfare Assistance Payments Manual is violative of the federal statutory requirement that aid be "furnished with reasonable promptness to all eligible individuals," 42 U.S.C.A. § 602(a)(10), and is invalid. Accordingly, the defendants will be enjoined from denying or discontinuing AFDC assistance to members of the class in this action on the basis that they have failed to meet the requirements of the subject regulatory section.

Assignment # 48

a. If § 602(a)(17)(A)(i) does not mean that noncooperation can lead to ineligibility, what does it mean? Was *Doe v. Flowers* correctly decided?

b. Could the West Virginia Department of Welfare publish the following notice in a newspaper: "Mary Jones and her son have applied for AFDC benefits. In order to process this application, we need to contact the father of this child. Please call 363–7159 if you have any information as to his whereabouts."

c. Could the West Virginia Department of Welfare refuse to give AFDC benefits to any parent who refuses to come to the agency and apply in person? Assume that the parent is a healthy individual who prefers to apply on the phone? If benefits are denied, would the agency be imposing an additional condition of eligibility? If not, how does this differ from *Doe v. Flowers?*

Assignment # 49

Statute: § 1304. Whoever broadcasts by means of any radio or television station, or whoever, operating any such station, knowingly permits the broadcasting of, any advertisement of or information concerning any lottery offering prizes dependent in whole or in part upon lot or chance shall be fined not more than $1000.

Regulation: § 15. Programs falling within the ban of § 1304 shall include programs where a prize is awarded to any person whose selection is dependent in whole or part upon lot or chance, if as a condition of winning or competing for such prize the winner is required to be listening to or viewing the program or to correctly answer a question that is broadcast over the air.

The Federal Communications Commission has issued § 15 as part of its responsibility of administering § 1304. The agency has charged the producers of "Stop the Music" with violating § 1304 as interpreted by § 15. The radio version of the program calls listeners at random from the phone book. The person called is required to identify the title of a song. If he or she was not listening to the radio at the time the song was played, the host hums or sings part of it on the phone. A cash prize is awarded for the right answer. Is the agency correct?

Assignment # 50

In each of the following situations, determine whether the regulation is validly based on the statute.

a. Statute: § 42. All income shall be subject to taxation.

Regulation: § 16.444(a). The reasonable value of all employer-provided Christmas parties shall be proportionately included within the income of every attending employee for purposes of taxation under § 42.

b. Statute: § 702. Alimony payments, but not child support payments, are deductible to the payor.

Regulation: § 1.702(s). If a payment is made to an ex-spouse which does not specifically designate what portion of the payment is for alimony and what portion is for child support, the Internal Revenue Service shall treat the entire payment as child support.

c. Statute: § 36. Grazing on public lands of the United States shall be prohibited unless special permission is obtained therefor from the Secretary of the Interior.

Regulation: § 9. Authorization to graze on public lands of the United States shall be granted by the Secretary of the Interior if the applicant is a full-time farmer and pays a permission fee of 50 cents per animal per day.

Chapter Fourteen

Legislative Drafting

We now shift perspective from the *interpreter* of statutes to the *drafter* of statutes. This shift does not take us away from the theme of legislative *analysis*. The two perspectives substantially reinforce the basic theme of analysis. The interpreter of legislative language must always ask, "why was it written this way?" while one of the preoccupations of the drafter is "how will this be interpreted?" The fundamentals of analysis will help answer both questions.

Outline of Chapter

A. Introduction
B. Preparation: Background Research
C. Some Mechanics
D. Arrangement/Organization of the Law
E. Definitions
F. Consistency
G. Contingencies and Provisos
H. Tense

I. Mood
J. Shall and May
K. Voice
L. Use of Singular and Plural
M. Action Verbs
N. Directness
O. Pronoun Reference
P. Such and Said
Q. And/Or
R. Any, Each, Every, etc.
S. Hyphenated Words
T. Numbers
U. Choice of Language
V. Sexism in Language

Section A. Introduction [1]

Bill drafting must have the accuracy of engineering, for it is law engineering; it must have the detail and the consistency of architecture, for it is law architecture.[2]

The important idea in legislative drafting is to say what you mean accurately, cohesively, clearly, and economically. Substance comes before form, but the two run together. You start by determining the needs to be filled, look for specific answers, arrange the answers in a coherent plan, and express the results as clearly and simply as the complexities of the plan allow. Form is important to substance because ambiguity and confused expression tend to defeat the purposes of the legislation. Substance and arrangement are im-

---

1. Adapted from *A Manual for Drafting Federal Legislation, Drafting Manual for the Army and Air Force Codes*, 11 Federal Bar Journal 238 (1950); French, B., *Council of the District of Columbia Legislative Drafting Manual, Revised Edition*, 25 Howard Law Journal 731 (1982); Michigan Legislative Service Bureau, *Drafting Manual for Administrative Rules* (1980); U.S. Government Printing Office, *Style Manual* (Rev. Ed. 1973); Office of the Federal Register, Document Drafting Handbook (Rev. Ed. 1980).

2. Kennedy, *Drafting Bills for the Minnesota Legislature* (1946).

portant to form because no amount of language "simplification" will make simple sense out of a statute whose underlying approach is confused. Clarity and simplicity, therefore, begin with straightforward thinking and end with straightforward expression.

Section B. Preparation: Background Research

Once an idea for a statute has been developed, a great deal of background research is needed. There is a twofold direction to the research: what is the current law in your jurisdiction on the subject matter of the proposed statute, and how have the legislatures of other jurisdictions handled this subject matter.

You start at home with the cry from someone that "there otta be a law!" The demand can be for the passage of a new law (e.g., create an agency with responsibility for cleaning up river pollution), or for changes in the current law (e.g., amend the tax code to allow a deduction for college expenses). Suppose, for example, that a legislator or a constituent group is calling for a change in the law of the insanity defense in criminal cases. A defendant who attempted to kill the president has just been found not guilty by reason of insanity. Widespread publicity and criticism follow the acquittal.

The first trip of the drafter is to the law library. You must become an expert on the area of insanity by carefully reading:

- every provision in your state constitution on the subject;
- every statute of your state legislature on the subject;
- every major court opinion on the subject by the courts of your state;
- every opinion of the state attorney general on the subject;
- every regulation on the subject from administrative agencies;

- every major federal law on the subject (constitution, court opinion, regulation, etc.);

- every major scholarly commentary on the subject in treatises, law reviews, and bar association journals;

- every major study on the subject from agencies, bar associations, public interest groups such as unions, police associations, medical societies, social scientists, the academic community, trade associations, lobbyists;

- every major proposal on the subject from groups that have proposed legislative action such as the National Conference of Commissioners on Uniform State Laws, the Council of State Governments, the American Law Institute, the American Bar Association.

In addition, you must determine what other legislatures have done in this area. What statutes do they have on the subject? What are the differences among them? Why were they passed? What has the experience been under the statutes? What strengths and weaknesses have been identified? What improvement is needed? What has been the response of the courts, the agencies charged with enforcement, the lawyers, the social scientists, the media, the public?

From all of this reading, study, and contact, you are now in a much better position to advise whether it is true that "there otta be a law," and if so, what shape it should take. This background research will equip you to help the policy makers articulate precisely what it is they want to do. You can formulate questions and options that will help them identify:

- whether there is a need for a new law;

- what purpose it will serve;

- who will benefit from the law, who will be disadvantaged;

- what the costs of administering the law will probably be;

- what the likely response to the law will be from the courts, the bureaucracy, and the public.

Section C. Some Mechanics

Legislatures differ as to the requirements for the format and structure of bills, i.e., proposed legislation. The requirements may be imposed by the governing constitution, by statutes, or by custom and tradition. While the guidelines to be discussed here are generally applicable, the specifications for each individual legislature would have to be checked for any drafting task.

A BILL

To amend the Universal Military Training and Service Act, as amended, so as to provide that persons inducted into the Armed Forces of the United States under such Act shall not be assigned to duty in southeast Asia unless they volunteer for such duty.

Be it enacted by the Senate and House of Representatives of the United States of America in Congress Assembled, That the Universal Military Training and Service Act, as amended (50 App. U.S.C. 451–471), is amended by adding at the end thereof a new section as follows:

Sec. 22. No person inducted into the Armed Forces of the United States under this Act shall be assigned to duty or required to perform service in southeast Asia unless such person volunteers for assignment to duty in such area.

(a) Long Title At the beginning of the bill there is a *long title* which states the subject matter of the proposed law in a concise but comprehensive manner, e.g., "To establish a National Commission for the Preservation of . . . "; "To amend the Universal Military Training and Service Act . . . ." In some jurisdictions, the long title is required for the validity of the law, if enacted. Other requirements may also be imposed, e.g., statement of special effective dates (p. 143), statement of whether the statute will contain penalty provisions. The long title alerts everyone to the function of the proposed law. While the long title is usually not part of the law itself, it is frequently consulted as part of the legislative history (p. 97) of the statute when an issue arises as to the legislature's intent in passing the statute. When the bill is enacted into law, the long title is often dropped and does not appear in the statutory code compilation.

(b) Enabling Clause In most jurisdictions, the only part of a bill that can become law is what follows the enabling clause which begins, "Be it enacted by . . . ."

(c) Short Title Many statutes have popular names that are called *short* titles, e.g., the Civil Rights Act, the Interest Stabilization Act of 1980, the Universal Military Training and Service Act. The short title may be found within the enabling clause or within one of the first sections in the body of the statute itself. An amendment to a statute may or may not have a short title, but the statute it amends will usually have one. At the end of the collection of statutes in the code there will often be a Table of Statutes by Popular Name which will allow you to locate a statute when you know only the short title.

(d) Headnotes, Captions, or Section Headings for Individual Sections At the beginning of each section of the statute, there is often a headnote or caption that briefly states the topic or theme of that section. For § 2305, the headnote (in darker print) is "Full and limited warranting of a consumer product":

> **§ 2305. Full and limited warranting of a consumer product**
>
> Nothing in this chapter shall prohibit the selling of a consumer product which has both full and limited warranties if such warranties are clearly and conspicuously differentiated.

The headnote is a convenient editorial flag that capsulizes the topic of each section. For most statutes, it is not part of the law itself unless it is clear that the legislature has adopted it.

(e) Purpose Clause At the beginning of the body of the statute, there occasionally is a purpose clause which states the policy behind the statute and perhaps some findings or conclusions of fact that prompted the legislature to pass the statute. In a more extensive way, it serves the same function as the long title, although unlike the latter, the purpose clause is part of the statute itself (see Figure 5).

Figure 5. Example of a Public Law

Public Law 93–438
93rd Congress, H. R. 11510
October 11, 1974

𝔄𝔫 𝔄𝔠𝔱

To reorganize and consolidate certain functions of the Federal Government in a new Energy Research and Development Administration and in a new Nuclear Regulatory Commission in order to promote more efficient management of such functions.

Be it enacted by the Senate and House of Representatives of the United States of America in Congress assembled.

SHORT TITLE

SECTION 1. This Act may be cited as the "Energy Reorganization Act of 1974".

DECLARATION OF PURPOSE

SEC. 2. (a) The Congress hereby declares that the general welfare and the common defense and security require effective action to develop, and increase the efficiency and reliability of use of, all energy sources to meet the needs of present and future generations, to increase the productivity of the national economy and strengthen its position in regard to international trade, to make the Nation self-sufficient in energy, to advance the goals of restoring, protecting, and enhancing environmental quality, and to assure public health and safety.

(b) The Congress finds that, to best achieve these objectives, improve Government operations, and assure the coordinated and effective development of all energy sources, it is necessary to establish an Energy Research and Development Administration to bring together and direct Federal activities relating to research and development on the various sources of energy, to increase the efficiency and reliability in the use of energy, and to carry out the performance of other functions, including but not limited to the Atomic Energy Commission's military and production activities and its general basic research activities. In establishing an Energy Research and Development Administration to achieve these objectives, the Congress intends that all possible sources of energy be developed consistent with warranted priorities.

(c) The Congress finds that it is in the public interest that the licensing and related regulatory functions of the Atomic Energy Commission be separated from the performance of the other functions of the Commission, and that this separation be effected in an orderly manner, pursuant to this Act, assuring adequacy of technical and other resources necessary for the performance of each.

(d) The Congress declares that it is in the public interest and the policy of Congress that small business concerns be given a reasonable opportunity to participate, insofar as is possible, fairly and equitably in grants, contracts, purchases, and other Federal activities relating to research, development, and demonstration of sources of energy efficiency, and utilization and conservation of energy. In carrying out this policy, to the extent practicable, the Administrator shall consult with the Administrator of the Small Business Administration.

(e) Determination of priorities which are warranted should be based on such considerations as power-related values of an energy source, preservation of material resources, reduction of pollutants, export market potential (including reduction of imports), among others. On such a basis, energy sources warranting priority might include, but not be limited to, the various methods of utilizing solar energy.

The potential usefulness of such clauses to a determination of legislative intent is obvious. There are, however, dangers in their use, and some drafters recommend that they *not* be used. (They are not required.) The main danger is that they will not accurately reflect what the legislature did in the rest of the statute. The purpose clause, for example, may be underinclusive in that it does not appear to cover everything in the statute. Since the clause is very difficult to draft with precision, and may not be necessary in a statute whose purpose is otherwise clear, the safest course is to omit it unless a need for its presence can be justified for particular kinds of statutes.

(f) Severability Clause A statute may have numerous sections. What happens if a court declares one of these sections to be unconstitutional? Does the entire statute fall?

Legislatures often express their intent on this point by inserting a severability clause:

> § 503. If any provision of this Act or application thereof to any person or circumstance is held invalid, the invalidity does not affect other provisions or applications of the Act which can be given effect without the invalid provision or application, and to this end the provisions of this Act are severable.

If, on the other hand, the legislature wants the entire statute to die if *any* portion of it is declared invalid, or if *designated* portions are declared invalid, then this should be specified in the statute.

(g) Saving Clause If the legislature wants to make clear that the statute does not affect certain rights, remedies or privileges, a saving clause will be inserted. For example:

> § 862. This Act does not affect rights, duties, and privileges that vested, penalties that were incurred, and proceedings that were begun before its effective date.

(h) Effective Date It is often extremely important to know when a statute becomes effective. Statutes create or destroy rights, establish new penalties, institute new procedures, etc. The effective date of these changes is obviously critical for the individuals and institutions involved. If the statute is silent on the effective date, then a standard rule in the jurisdiction (perhaps established by the constitution) will set this date, e.g., on the day after it is adopted and signed by the chief executive. When the legislature does not want this rule to apply, then, of course, an alternative date is specified, usually at the very end of the statute in a separate section. Within certain limitations, the legislature has the power to give retroactive effect to its statutes as we saw in Chapter 11 (p. 146).

(i) Amendments Many statutes are amendments of other statutes. The conventional way to draft the amendment is to type the original statute, draw a thin line through words that are to be omitted, underline words that are to be added, and leave the rest of the original statute intact. For example:

§ 2068. Prohibited acts

(a) It shall be unlawful for any person to—

(1) manufacture for sale, ~~offer for sale,~~ distribute in commerce, or import <u>into the United States,</u> any consumer product which is not in conformity with an applicable consumer product safety standard under this chapter;

<u>(2) manufacture for sale, offer for sale, distribute in commerce, or import into the United States any consumer product which has been declared a banned hazardous product by a rule under this</u> . . . .

In § 2068(a)(1), the amendment strikes the words "offer for sale" and adds the words "into the United States". Section 2068(a)(2) is totally new. The rest of the words in the statute were in the original and are intended to survive the amendment.

Section D. Arrangement/Organization of the Law

a. One of the most fundamental problems in drafting is that of arrangement. The main idea is to make the final product as useful as possible. Carefully select the subjects to be covered and arrange them so that they can be found, understood, and referred to with the least possible effort.

b. In general, the subject groupings that are appropriate for a particular law depend upon the needs of the persons who will use the text of the law most. Arrange provisions relating primarily to administration from the viewpoint of the persons who will administer them. Arrange provisions relating primarily to the conduct, rights, privileges, or duties of persons not administering them from the viewpoint of the persons so affected. Consider not only *who* and *how many* will use a provision but *how often* they will use it.

c. The sections of a statute can often be divided into three main units which are presented after the purpose clause (p. 166) and the definitions section, if any, at the beginning of the statute (p. 176):

(1) The Substantive Provisions of the Statute

Here you present the heart of the statute—the reason the statute was passed. What right, duty, or privilege is being created, modified, or eliminated? Are taxes being raised, gun control imposed, no-fault insurance curtailed, marijuana decriminalized, worker's compensation extended to farmers?

(2) The Administrative Provisions of the Statute

What agency has responsibility for administering the statute? What are the powers of this agency? What are the qualifications of the person who will be in charge? What staff will be available to this person? What will the salary levels be? How will citizens come into contact with the agency? Through an application process? What procedures will govern the process within the agency? Does the agency have the power of subpoena? Does it have the power to write regulations implementing the statute? What reports must the agency prepare on its operations?

(3) Sanctions

What sanctions will exist for violating the statute and how will these sanctions be imposed? Criminal sanctions of a fine, imprisonment or both? Civil sanctions allowing the injured party to sue for damages in court? Can a court injunction be obtained? A temporary restraining order? Will a license be revoked or suspended? Will compliance efforts be required? Will the party violating the statute be subject to monitoring and publicity?

d. Generally, the best arrangements require the least page-turning. Avoid any arrangement, for instance, that requires substantially more cross-references between chapters than is required by an alternative arrangement offering equal or better findability, clarity, and usability.

e. Do not state the same rule of law at more than one place.

f. Treat functionally indivisible subjects at a single place. Do not fragment them.

g. For identification it is usually desirable to designate each paragraph of text by a letter or number. Simple enumerations, whether or not in tabular form, may or may not be designated.

h. When designating paragraph groupings within a section, follow these conventions: For subdivisions of a section (called "subsections"), use "(a)", "(b)", "(c)", etc. For subdivisions of a subsection (called "paragraphs"), use "(1)", "(2)", "(3)", etc. For subdivisions of a paragraph (called "subparagraphs"), use "(A)", "(B)", "(C)", etc. Avoid further subdivisions wherever possible. Where an additional designated breakdown is necessary, use "(i)", "(ii)", "(iii)", etc.

i. When designating a tabulation in a section that has no subsections, use "(1)", "(2)", "(3)", etc.

j. When organizing sections, subsections, and other subdivisions of the text, try to use a single principle of classification at any level of classification.

k. In a series, list, or other enumeration, introductory language that applies to more than one item named must apply to all. Departures from this principle constitute "bastard enumeration."

Don't say	*Say*
The several States, Territories, and the District of Columbia	The several States and Territories, and the District of Columbia
	or
	The several States, the several Territories, and the District of Columbia

(a) When used in this title, the term—	(a) When used in this title, the term—
(1) Army means . . .	(1) Army means . . .
(2) Regular Army means . . .	(2) Regular Army means . . .
(3) The Secretary shall determine . . .	(b) The Secretary shall determine . . .

In the second example note that (a)(3) is not consistent with (a)(1) and (a)(2). Hence (a)(3) has been reorganized as a new classification: (b).

l. If it is necessary to incorporate a large amount of material into one rule, you should consider subdividing the rule in a series of independently numbered statements. For example, it is preferable to divide the text of a single rule that describes the steps in applying for a license into a series of subrules, with each subrule describing a separate step. Compare the following drafts:

FIRST DRAFT

§ 338.1906.   Application for license

An applicant for a license shall submit to the Board an application on forms prepared and furnished by the department. An application shall be accompanied by the statutory fee and shall be made under oath. Each question shall be answered in its entirety. An incomplete application shall be completed and resubmitted to the Board within 15 days after the date of the Board's request. Failure to comply is grounds for denial of the application and forfeiture of application fees already paid.

SECOND DRAFT

§ 338.1906.   Application for license

(1) An applicant for a license shall submit to the Board an application on forms prepared and furnished by the department.

(2) An application shall be accompanied by the statutory fee and shall be made under oath. Each question shall be answered in its entirety.

(3) An incomplete application shall be completed and resubmitted to the Board within 15 days after the date of the Board's request.

(4) Failure to comply with subsection (3) is grounds for denial of the application and forfeiture of application fees already paid.

The second draft is preferable because the separate steps in the application process are more readily discernible. Note also that in the first draft there is some ambiguity as to whether the phrase "failure to comply" in the last sentence refers only to the next-to-the last sentence or to the entire statute. The second draft allows us to remove this ambiguity with ease by making a specific reference to the numbered subrule to which the phrase applies.

Section E. Definitions

a. Avoid unnecessary definitions in the statute. The main purpose of a definition is to obtain clarity without needless repetition.

b. There are three kinds of useful legal "definitions":

(1) Nominal
(e.g., The term "fracture" means break.). Here you equate a term to a more familiar term. This is not strictly a definition, but it is frequently helpful in conveying the meaning of a term.

(2) Connotative
(e.g., The term "grade" means a step or degree, in a graduated scale of department rank, which is established and designated by law or regulation.). Here you define the subject in terms of (A) a broader class into which it falls (i.e., a step or degree in a graduated scale of department rank), and (B) the features that distinguish the subject from all other subjects in that class (i.e., established and designated by law or regulation). This is a true definition.

(3) Denotative
(e.g., The term "Army" includes the Regular Army, the National Guard of the United States, the Organized Reserve Corps, . . .). Here you explain the subject by listing some or all of its component parts.

c. A true definition must not contain, directly or indirectly, the word or phrase being defined.

d. If you cannot make a connotative definition sufficiently unambiguous or concrete, you may want to bolster it by listing the components that are in doubt. But do not make the list itself an exhaustive definition (by using the words "means" or "consists of") unless you withdraw the other definition. Concurrent definitions are likely to become conflicting definitions. Handle the problem as shown in the following example:

Example:

> The term "grade" means a step or degree, in a graduated scale of department rank, which is established and designated by law or regulation. It includes such steps as those of colonel, lieutenant, sergeant, private, recruit, and cadet.

e. Do not define a word in a sense that conflicts with accepted usage. Use the word in its normal sense and make the provision in which it appears directly state the substantive result you want. If you adopt a fiction, label it plainly by using "as if" language.

Example:

> *Don't Say:* In this chapter, the term "colonel" means an individual who is a colonel, lieutenant colonel, or major.
>
> *Say:* Lieutenant colonels and majors have the same rights, privileges, and duties as this chapter provides for colonels.
>
> *Or:* In this chapter, lieutenant colonels and majors shall be treated as if they were colonels.

f. A denotative definition should show whether it is intended to be exhaustive or partial. In the first case, use the word "means"; in the second, the word "includes." Never use the ambiguous expression "means and includes."

g. Do not insert substantive rules in definitions. Definitions are not commands.

> *Don't Say:* "Daytime" means the hours between 7 a.m. and 10 p.m. and service of process shall occur during the daytime.
>
> *Say:* § 2. "Daytime" means the hours between 7 a.m. and 10 p.m.
>
> § 2(a) Service of process shall occur during the daytime.

h. Use the indicative not the imperative mood in your definitions.

Don't Say: In this section, "explosive" shall mean . . . .

Say: In this section, "explosive" means . . . .

i. Place definitions where they are most easily found and used. A word or phrase that is used only in one place should be defined at that place. (In this section, the word "vacate" means . . . .) A word or phrase that is used throughout a chapter should be defined at the beginning of the chapter. (In this chapter, "unilateral" means . . . .) A word or phrase that is used throughout the statute should be defined at the beginning of the entire statute. (In this act, "reasonable" means . . . .)

j. Many statutory codes have interpretation or construction statutes, often at the beginning of the code. These statutes will sometimes provide standard definitions that are to be used throughout the code unless otherwise indicated. There is no need to repeat any of these definitions elsewhere in the code. The following are examples of such standard definitions or rules of interpretation:

1. Words importing the singular include the plural.

2. Words importing the plural include the singular.

3. Words importing the masculine gender include the feminine.

4. The present tense includes the future.

5. The terms "person" and "whoever" include corporations, companies, associations, firms, partnerships, societies, and joint stock companies.

6. The term "officer" includes any person authorized by law to perform the duties of the office.

7. The term "oath" includes affirmation; the term "sworn" includes affirmed.

8. The term "writing" includes printing, typewriting, and reproductions of visual symbols by photographing, multigraphing, mimeographing, manifolding, or otherwise.

9. The word "vessel" includes every description of water-craft or other artificial contrivance used, or capable of being used, as a means of transportation on water.

10. The word "vehicle" includes every description of carriage or other artificial contrivance used, or capable of being used, as a means of transportation on land.

11. The term "company" or "association," when used in reference to a corporation, is treated as including its successors and assigns.

Section F. Consistency

a. Be consistent and uniform in the use of language.

b. Because different words are presumed to refer to different things, do not use different words to denote the same thing ("elegant variation"). Variation for the sake of variation has no place in drafting. Using a synonym or a synonymous expression rather than repeating the precise term you intend can confuse the reader.

> *Don't Say:* Each motor vehicle owner shall register his or her car with the Automobile Division of the Metropolitan Police Department.

> *If You Mean:* Each automobile owner shall register his or her automobile with the Automobile Division of the Metropolitan Police Department.

c. Be consistent in organization. If two sections are similar in substance, try to arrange them similarly.

Section G. Contingencies and Provisos

a. Ordinarily, state the circumstances in which the rule is to apply before you state the rule itself. Do not, however, start a sentence with an exception if you can conveniently avoid it.

Examples:

> If on the date specified for retirement or discharge the officer has completed 30 or more years' service, he or she shall be retired.

> Whenever the Secretary finds that there is an excessive number of officers in any grade, he or she may convene a board of five members of the Regular Army . . . .

b. On the other hand, if the circumstances in which the rule is to apply involve numerous contingencies or conditions, you may find it desirable to state the rule first. In such a case, it may be appropriate to put an exception at the beginning.

Example:

> Except as provided in subsection (b), a member of a reserve component is entitled to retired pay if the member:
>
> (1) is at least 60 years old;
>
> (2) has completed 30 or more years of satisfactory federal service;
>
> (3) served the last 9 of those years as a member of a reserve component; and
>
> (4) is not receiving retired pay for military service or retainer pay as a transferred member of the Fleet Reserve.

c. Where there are a number of unwieldy contingencies, alternatives, or requirements, make each a separate clause (see example above).

d. Use the following drafting guidelines to avoid an expression such as "provided however":

1. To introduce a qualification or limitation to a rule, use "but".

2. To introduce an exception to a rule, use "except that".

3. To introduce a condition to a rule, use "if".

4. If the qualification, exception, or condition is a complete thought, start a new sentence or subsection.

e. Do not include two provisos in the same sentence.

Section H. Tense

a. Use the present tense. The operation of the law is continuous and therefore always in the present tense.

Don't say: A permit shall not be granted until the applicant has *filed* an organization report.

Say: A permit shall not be granted until the applicant *files* an organization report.

b. Whenever possible, avoid the future tense. Use "shall" for requirements and prohibitions.

c. To express a condition precedent, use the past tense to state facts precedent to the operation of the law, and the present tense for facts concurrent with the law.

Example:

If an applicant has qualified for worker's compensation on the date specified in § 34, the applicant is entitled . . . .

d. If it is necessary that a provision include past as well as future events, use the present tense but include before the appropriate verb the phrase, ". . . , before and after this Act [or title, part, section, etc.] is enacted, . . . ".

Section I. Mood

a. The words "shall" and "shall not" normally imply that to accomplish the purpose of the provision someone must act or refrain from acting. Drafters frequently use these words merely to declare a legal result, rather than to prescribe a rule of conduct. In many of these instances, the word "shall" is not only unnecessary but involves a circumlocution in thought because the purpose of the provision is achieved in the very act of declaring the legal result. In declaratory provisions, therefore, it is preferable, wherever possible, to use the indicative rather than the imperative mood.

Don't Say	*Say*
(1) "The term 'person' shall mean . . ."	(1) "The term 'person' means . . ."

Don't Say—Continued	*Say*—Continued
(2) "The equipment shall remain the property of the United States."	(2) "The equipment remains the property of the United States."
(3) "No person shall be entitled . . ."	(3) "No person is entitled . . ."

b. Avoid the subjunctive.

Don't Say: . . . if it be damaged . . . .

Say: . . . if it is damaged . . . .

Section J. Shall and May

a. "Shall" indicates an affirmative duty. If an obligation to act is imposed, use "shall". You are using the word "shall" properly if you can substitute the phrase "has the duty to" for "shall" and still retain the meaning intended.

Example:

The agency head shall establish a board of review before January 19, 1979.

b. Do not use the word "shall" to declare a legal result or to state a condition.

Don't Say: The liquid shall be at a temperature of 70 degrees fahrenheit when the test is administered.

Say: The chemist shall ensure that the temperature of the liquid is 70 degrees fahrenheit when the test is administered.

c. "May" is permissive in character; it should be used only to express a power or a privilege, not a right. "May" means "is authorized to" or "shall have the power to". Do not use "may" to express a duty to act or to refrain from acting.

Section K. Voice

a. Wherever possible, use the active voice instead of the passive.

Don't Say	*Say*
(1) The chief of each branch shall be appointed by the President from officers who	(1) The president shall appoint the chief of each branch from officers who . . . .
(2) A written examination shall be passed by an applicant for a license.	(2) An applicant for a license shall pass a written examination.
(3) An affidavit shall be filed by the corporation with the Commission.	(3) A corporation shall file an affidavit with the Commission.

b. In sections conferring powers or privileges or imposing duties, using the active voice will help to avoid vagueness by forcing the drafter to name, as the subject of the sentence, the person in whom the power or privilege is vested or upon whom the duty is imposed.

Don't Say: The vehicle shall be returned in good working order.

Say: The chief maintenance officer shall return the vehicle in good working order.

Section L. Use of Singular and Plural

a. To the extent your meaning allows, use the singular instead of the plural. This will avoid the question whether the plural applies to each individual member of the class or to the class as a whole.

Don't Say	*Say*
"The Secretary shall establish officers' retired lists for the components named in § 1304."	"The Secretary shall establish an officers' retired list for each component named in § 1304."
	unless you mean
	"The Secretary shall establish officers' retired lists for each of the components named in § 1304."

Say—Continued

or

"The Secretary shall establish officers' retired lists, each of which shall be for all of the components named in § 1304."

b. If it is necessary to use the plural, you can change to the singular, wherever desirable, by using the device shown in the following example:

Example:

Officers who have passed the examination shall be retired as provided in § 704. *Such an* officer may . . . .

Section M. Action Verbs

Wherever possible, draft your sentences to use "action" verbs instead of participles, gerunds, and other noun or adjective forms. Action verbs are shorter and more direct.

Don't Say	*Say*
give consideration to	consider
give recognition to	recognize
have knowledge of	know
have need of	need
in the determination of	to determine
is applicable	applies
is dependent on	depends on
is in attendance at	attends
make an appointment of	appoint
make application	apply
make payment	pay
make provision for	provide for

Section N. Directness

Where the same idea can be accurately expressed either positively or negatively, express it positively.

Don't Say	*Say*
(1) This section does not apply to officers under 60 years of age.	(1) This section applies only to officers who have become 60 years of age.
(2) Air Force officers other than those with no children may	(2) Air Force officers with children may . . . .

Section O. Pronoun Reference

a. Use pronouns only where the nouns to which the pronouns refer are unmistakably clear. The use of pronouns with ambiguous referents can confuse the meaning of a sentence.

b. If the pronoun could refer to more than one person or object in a sentence, repeat the name of the person or object to avoid the ambiguity.

Don't Say: After the Administrator appoints a Deputy Assistant, he or she shall supervise the . . . . [Who does the supervising? The Administrator or the Deputy? If the latter is intended, then:]

Say: After the Administrator appoints a Deputy Assistant, the Deputy Assistant shall supervise the . . . .

Section P. Such and Said

a. Generally, do not use the word "such". (For an exception see p. 182, Section L.) Use the more common article or pronouns, "the", "that", "those", "it", or "them" to refer back to something in the text.

Don't Say: The agency head shall file a report within 24 hours. Such report shall include . . . .

Say: The agency head shall file a report within 24 hours. The report shall include . . . .

b. If you mean "for example", use the phrase "such as" or "such a".

Example:

A liberal arts major takes courses in the humanities such as classical literature, history, and philosophy.

c. Do not use the word "said". Instead, use "the", "that", or "those" to refer back to something in the text.

Don't Say: The contractor shall insure against any loss caused by blasting. The contractor shall purchase said insurance from a reliable insurance company.

Say: The contractor shall insure against any loss caused by blasting. The contractor shall purchase the insurance from a reliable insurance company.

Section Q. And/Or

Do not use "and/or" since the combination of conjunctive ("and") and disjunctive ("or") indicates an alternative. Decide whether "and" or "or" is appropriate for the sentence and use that word alone. Use "or both" when necessary to include items both individually and together.

Example:

Violation of any provision of this Act is punishable by a fine of $100 or imprisonment of 6 months, or both.

Section R. Any, Each, Every, etc.

a. Use adjectives such as "each," "every," "any," "all," "no," and "some" (technically known as "pronominal indefinite adjectives") only where necessary.

b. If the subject of the sentence is plural, it is almost never necessary to use this kind of adjective (e.g., Majors of the Regular Army shall . . . .; Majors of the Regular Army may not . . . .).

c. If the subject of the sentence is singular, use the pronominal indefinite only when the article "a" or "the" is inadequate, as when the use of "a" would allow the unintended interpretation that the obligation is to be discharged (or the privilege exhausted) by applying it to a single member of the class instead of to all of them. If it is necessary to use a pronominal indefinite, follow these conventions:

1. If a right, privilege, or power is conferred, use "any" (e.g., Any major of the Regular Army may .   . .).

2. If an obligation to act is imposed, use "each" (e.g., Each major of the Regular Army shall .   . .).

3. If a right, privilege, or power is abridged, or an obligation to abstain from acting is imposed, use "no" (e.g., No major of the Regular Army may .   . .; No major of the Regular Army shall .   . .).

Section S. Hyphenated Words

a. Adjectives composed of two or more words are usually hyphenated when they precede a noun.

Examples:

    interest-bearing account

    over-the-counter sales

    moderate-income person

b. If the first word of a compound adjective is an adverb ending in "ly", the combination should not be hyphenated.

Examples:

    publicly owned building

    legally required action

    municipally owned building

c. Numbers from 21 to 99 are hyphenated when spelled out.

Examples:

thirty-eight dollars

one hundred fifty-five dollars

d. Fractions are hyphenated when spelled out unless they contain a hyphenated number in the numerator or denominator.

Examples:

a two-thirds interest

two thirty-thirds

twenty-three one hundreds

Section T. Numbers

a. Express cardinal numbers as figures, except at the beginning of a sentence.

Examples:

The licensee shall retain the report for not less than 6 years.

Two persons shall be stationed at each intersection.

b. Spell out ordinal numbers.

Example:

A report of the transaction shall be submitted to the bureau on the fifteenth day after the transaction is completed.

c. If an ordinal number is followed by a month, such as "on the first day of May," convert the phrase to read "on May 1."

Section U. Choice of Language

1. Forbidden Words

Avoid the following terms altogether:

above (as an adjective)

aforesaid

afore-mentioned

and/or (say "A or B, or both")

before-mentioned

provided that

said (as a substitute for "the," "that," or "those")

same (as a substitute for "it," "he," "him," etc.)

to wit

whatsoever

whensoever

wheresoever

2. Circumlocutions

a. Avoid pairs of words having the same effect:

alter and change

any and all

authorize and empower

by and with[3]

each and all

each and every

final and conclusive

from and after

full and complete

full force and effect

made and entered into

null and void

order and direct

over and above

sole and exclusive

type and kind

unless and until

---

3. For constitutional appointments, the phrase "by and with the advice and consent of the Senate" is a term of art and should not be changed.

b. Avoid pairs of words one of which includes the other (use the broader or narrower term as the substance requires):

authorize and direct

means and includes

c. Avoid expressions such as:

none whatever

make application, make a determination

shall be considered [or deemed] to be, may be treated as, have the effect of (unless a fiction is intended)

3. Preferred Expressions

a. Unless there are special reasons to the contrary:

Don't Say	Say
(1) accorded	(1) given
(2) adequate number of	(2) enough
(3) admit of	(3) allow
(4) afforded	(4) given
(5) all of the	(5) all the
(6) a person is prohibited from	(6) a person shall not
(7) approximately	(7) about
(8) at least	(8) not less than (when referring to two or more)
(9) at such time as	(9) when
(10) attains the age of ____	(10) becomes ____ years of age
(11) attempt (as a verb)	(11) try
(12) at the time	(12) when
(13) by means of	(13) by
(14) calculate	(14) compute
(15) category	(15) kind, class, group
(16) cause it to be done	(16) have it done
(17) contiguous to	(17) next to
(18) corporation organized under the laws of Ohio	(18) Ohio corporation
(19) deem	(19) consider
(20) does not operate to	(20) does not

Don't Say—Continued	*Say*—Continued
(21) during such time as	(21) while
(22) during the course of	(22) during
(23) endeavor (as a verb)	(23) try
(24) enter into a contract with	(24) to contract with
(25) evince	(25) show
(26) expiration	(26) end
(27) for the duration of	(27) during
(30) for the purpose of holding (or other gerund)	(30) to hold (or comparable infinitive)
(31) for the reason that	(31) because
(32) forthwith	(32) immediately
(33) in accordance with	(33) pursuant to, under
(34) in case	(34) if
(35) in cases in which	(35) when, where (say "whenever" or "wherever" only when you need to emphasize the exhaustive or recurring applicability of the rule)
(36) in order to	(36) to
(37) in sections 2023 to 2039 inclusive	(37) in sections 2013 to 2039
(38) in the case of	(38) [see (35) above]
(39) in the event of	(39) if
(40) in the event that	(40) if
(41) in the interest of	(41) for
(42) is able to	(42) can
(43) is applicable	(43) applies
(44) is authorized to	(44) may
(45) is binding upon	(45) binds
(46) is directed to	(46) shall
(47) is empowered to	(47) may
(48) is entitled (in the sense of "has the name")	(48) is called
(49) is entitled to	(49) may
(50) is hereby authorized and it shall be his duty to	(50) shall

Don't Say—Continued	*Say*—Continued
(51) is hereby authorized to	(51) shall
(52) is not prohibited from	(52) may
(53) is permitted to	(53) may
(54) is required to	(54) shall
(55) is unable to	(55) cannot
(56) it is directed	(56) shall
(57) it is his duty to	(57) shall
(58) it is the duty of	(58) shall
(59) it shall be lawful	(59) may
(60) it shall be unlawful for a person to	(60) a person shall not
(61) no later than June 30, 1981	(61) before July 1, 1983
(62) on or after July 1, 1984	(62) after June 30, 1984
(63) on or before June 30, 1985	(63) before July 1, 1985
(64) on the part of	(64) by
(65) or, in the alternative	(65) or
(66) paragraph (5) of sub-section (a) of section 2097	(66) section 2097(a)(5)
(67) per annum	(67) a year
(68) per centum	(68) percent
(69) period of time	(69) use period *or* time
(70) provision of law	(70) law
(71) render (in the sense of give)	(71) give
(72) State of Massachu-setts	(72) Massachusetts
(73) subsequent to	(73) after
(74) suffer (in the sense of permit)	(74) permit
(75) under the provisions of	(75) under
(76) until such time as	(76) until

b. Do not, however, change a term of art (p. 94), merely because it is found in the "Don't Say" column.

Section V. Sexism in Language

Avoid gender-specific language when the intent is to refer to both sexes. If neutral language is not available, rewrite the sentence to try to avoid the problem.

Gender-Specific Language	*Gender-Neutral Alternatives*
(1) business man	(1) executive, member of the business community
(2) chairman	(2) chairperson, chair
(3) draftsman	(3) drafter
(4) husband, wife	(4) spouse
(5) man (noun)	(5) person, human, humankind
(6) manhours	(6) worker hours
(7) mankind	(7) humanity
(8) manpower	(8) work force, personnel
(9) workman's compensation	(9) worker's compensation

Assignment # 51

Draft a "law" or regulation on smoking in the building where you are now studying. Assume that you cannot impose an absolute ban throughout the building. Cover topics such as where it will be allowed; where prohibited, time periods; different kinds of smoking (cigarettes, cigars, pipes); who must comply (students, teachers, administrators, clerical staff, maintenance staff) sanctions; who has responsibility for administering the law; procedural rights of alleged violators, etc.

Assignment # 52

Interview an administrative officer or teacher, or student, or secretary, or janitor at your school. Ask this person to identify a problem that the school is having in some aspect of administration. Draft a "law" or regulation to resolve this problem. Try to select a problem that is relatively narrow in scope.

Assignment # 53

Below you will find a number of topics or broad policy objectives which will be the basis of legislation that you will draft. You do not have to cover the entire topic or objective in your statute; you can carve out an area that would be appropriate for what you want to design. For purposes of this assignment, you do not have to do any background research. Assume that no prior law exists; you are writing on a clean slate in the sense that the legislature (of which you are a member) has never before tried to accomplish what you want to do in your statute.

a. Decriminalizing the use of heroin.

b. Preventing another Viet Nam.

c. Establishing a right to die.

d. Defining property and support rights of gay people who live together.

e. Preventing nuclear war.

f. Legalizing polygamy.

g. Establishing a system for national referenda on issues.

Appendix A

Selected Research
Checklists on Legislation

Checklist 1. Finding Court Opinions
Interpreting Statutes

a. Find the statute in the annotated code. Check the "Notes to Decisions" after the statute for summaries of court opinions interpreting the statute.

> **i.** Check pocket part of volume for later cases.

> **ii.** Check supplementary pamphlets at the end of the code for later cases.

b. Shepardize the statute. Find the set of *Shepard's Citations* covering the code containing your statute. Among the information Shepard's will give you will be court opinions that have mentioned or discussed the statute.

c. Check the digests. Go to the digests that cover the state that wrote the statute. (For federal statutes, go to the various federal digests, e.g., Federal Practice Digest, 2d.) Identify the major subject matters in the statute, e.g., worker's compensation. Use the index of the digests to find key topics and numbers on these subject matters. This will lead

193

you to small paragraph summaries of court opinions. See if
any of them treat your statute.

d. Check the ALRs. Use the index systems for the units of
American Law Reports: ALR, ALR 2d, ALR 3d, ALR 4th,
ALR Fed. In these indexes look for the subject matters of
your statute. This will lead you to annotations that summarize cases. See if any of them cover your statute. (For federal statutes, check the Table of Laws and Regulations cited
in ALR Fed in the volume called *ALR Fed Table of Cases, Laws,
Regs* which will lead you directly to annotations on particular
statutes of Congress.)

e. Check the legal periodicals. Use the major index systems
for this kind of literature: *Index to Legal Periodicals, Current Law
Index, Legal Resource Index.* In these indexes look for the subject
matters of your statute. This will lead you to periodical
literature. The footnotes in this literature may contain leads
to court opinions interpreting your statute. If you know the
popular name of your statute (p. 121), there are popular
name tables in the three index systems that will lead you
directly to periodical literature.

f. Check the treatises. For important statutes, there may be
entire books or sets of books devoted to your statute. The
treatises almost always give extensive references to opinions
interpreting the statute. Use the card catalog of your library
to locate such treatises.

g. Check the looseleaf services. Find out if there is one or
more looseleaf services on the subject matter of your statute.
One of the features of these services is a set of references to
court opinions interpreting statutes.

Checklist 2. Finding Regulations
Interpreting Statutes

a. Federal Regulations
   i. In the index volume of the *Code of Federal Regulations,*
   there is a table that will tell you what federal regulations
   are based on what federal statutes.

ii. Contact the federal agency to ask whether it has regulations implementing your statute.

iii. Check loose leaf services (see guideline g of Checklist 1). These services will often lead you to regulations on the statute.

iv. If you find cases interpreting the statute (see Checklist 1), the court will almost always tell you whether there are any regulations interpreting the statute.

b. State Regulations

i. Find out if there are any tables in the set of regulations for your state agency that will give cross references to the statutes on which the regulations are based.

ii. Contact the state agency to ask whether it has regulations implementing your statute.

iii. Same as guideline a(iii) above.

iv. Same as guideline a(iv) above.

Checklist 3. Tracing the Legislative History of a Federal Statute

a. Examine the historical data at the end of the statute in the United States Code (USC), and in the United States Code Annotated (USCA) and in the United States Code Service (USCS).

b. You will also find the PL number (Public Law number) of the statute at the end of the statute in USC/USCA/USCS. This PL number will be important for tracing legislative history. (Note that each amendment to a statute will have its own PL number.)

c. Step one in tracing the legislative history of a federal statute is to find out if the history has already been compiled by someone else. Ask your librarian. The Library of Congress compiles legislative histories. If the statute deals with a particular federal agency, check with the library or law department of that agency in Wash. D.C. or in the regional offices to see if it has compiled the legislative history. Also check with special interest groups or associations who are directly affected by the statute. They may have compiled the legislative history which might be available to you. Ask your librarian if there is a Union List of Legislative Histories, or something comparable, for your area. This List tells you what libraries have compiled legislative histories on federal statutes.

d. The following texts are useful in tracing the legislative history of federal statutes:

- U.S. Code Congressional & Administrative News (see Table 4)
- CCH Congressional Index
- Congressional Information Service (CIS) Annual and Legislative History Service
- Information Handling Service (legislative histories on microfiche)
- Digest of Public General Bills
- Congressional Record (see Index and the History of Bills and Resolutions for House and Senate)
- House and Senate Journals
- Congressional Quarterly
- Congressional Monitor
- Monthly Catalog of U.S. Documents

e. Contact both committees of Congress that considered the legislation to ask for leads to legislative history. (They may be able to send you committee reports, hearing transcripts, etc.)

f. Cases interpreting the statute sometimes give the legislative history of the statute. To find cases interpreting the statute see Checklist #1.

g. You may also find leads to the legislative history of a statute in legal periodical literature (see Checklist #1, guideline e), in treatises on the statute (see Checklist #1, guideline f), in loose leaf services on the statute (see Checklist #1, guideline g), and in annotations on the statute (see Checklist #1, guideline d).

h. Examine your statute in its session law form in Statutes at Large for possible leads.

Checklist 4. Tracing the Legislative History of a State Statute

a. Examine the historical data beneath the statute in the annotated statutory code. Amendments are usually listed there.

b. For an overview of codification information about your state, check the introductory pages in the first volume of the statutory code, or, the beginning of the volume where your statute is found, or, the beginning of the Shepard's volume that will enable you to shepardize the statutes of that state.

c. Ask your librarian if there is a book (usually called a legislative service) that covers your state legislature. If one exists, it will give the bill numbers of statutes, proposed amendments, names of sponsoring legislators, names of committees that considered the statute, etc. If such a text does not exist for your state, ask the librarian how someone finds the legislative history of a state statute in your state.

d. Contact the committees of both houses of the state legislature that considered the bill. Your local state representative or state senator might be able to help you identify what these committees were. If your statute is not too old, staff members on these committees may be able to give you leads to the legislative history of the statute. Ask if any committee reports were written. Ask about amendments, etc.

e. Ask your librarian (or a local politician) if there is a law revision commission for your state. If so, contact it for leads.

f. Is there a state law library in your area? If so, contact it for leads.

g. Check the law library and drafting office of the state legislature for leads.

h. Cases interpreting the statute sometimes give the legislative history of the statute. To find cases interpreting a statute, see Checklist # 1.

i. You may also find leads to the legislative history of a statute in legal periodical literature on the statute (see Checklist # 1, guideline *e*), in annotations on the statute (see Checklist # 1, guideline *d*), in treatises on the statute (see Checklist # 1, guideline *f*), and in looseleaf services on the statute (see Checklist # 1, guideline *g*).

References

Beer, An Annotated Guide to the Legal Literature of Michigan (1973)

Boner, A Reference Guide to Texas Law and Legal History: Sources and Documentation (1976).

Cohen and Berring, How to Find the Law, 8th Ed. (1983)

Davies, Research in Illinois Law (1954)

Fink, Research in California Law (1964)

French, Research in Florida Law (1965)

Gilmer, Legal Research, Writing and Advocacy (1978)

Henke, California Research Handbook, State and Federal (1971)

Henke, California Law Guide (1976)

Jacobstein and Mersky, Pollack's Fundamentals of Legal Research, 4th Ed. (1973)

Kavass, Guide to North Carolina Legal Research (1973)

Knudson, Wisconsin Legal Research Guide (1962)

Laska, Tennessee Legal Research Handbook (1977)

Lebowitz, Legal Bibliography and Research: An Outlined Manual on the Use of Law Books in the Texas and Federal Courts (1957)

Mills and Schultz, South Carolina Legal Research Methods (1976)

Poldervaart, Manual for Effective New Mexico Legal Research (1955)

Price, Bitner and Bysiewicz, Effective Legal Research, 4th Ed. (1979)

Rombauer, Legal Problem Solving: Analysis, Research and Writing 4th Ed. (1983)

Statsky, Legal Research, Writing and Analysis, 2d Ed. (1982)

Surrency, Research in Pennsylvania Law (1965)

Wallach, Louisiana Legal Research Manual (1972)

Werner, Manual for Prison Law Libraries (1976)

Appendix B

Standard Statutory Citation Forms

The following are examples of standard citation formats:

United States:	8 U.S.C. § 1158(b) (1976)
Alabama:	Ala.Code § 37 (1975)
Alaska:	Alaska Stat. § 1805 (1980)
Arizona:	Ariz.Rev.Stat.Ann. § 73 (1976)
Arkansas:	Ark.Stat.Ann. § 211 (1950)
California:	Cal.Penal Code § 90 (West 1970)
	Cal.Penal Code § 90 (Deering 1970)
Colorado:	Colo.Rev.Stat. § 100 (1960)
Connecticut:	Conn.Gen.Stat. § 95.1 (1976)
Delaware:	Del.Code Ann. tit. 4, § 38 (1980)
Dist. of Col.:	D.C.Code Ann. § 12–402 (1981)
Florida:	Fla.Stat. § 23 (1970)
	Fla.Stat.Ann. § 23 (West 1970)
Georgia:	Ga.Code § 657 (1980)
	Ga.Code Ann. § 657 (1980)
Hawaii:	Hawaii Rev.Stat. § 888 (1979)
Idaho:	Idaho Code § 45 (1979)

Illinois:	Ill.Rev.Stat. ch. 4, § 53 (1980) Ill.Ann.Stat. ch. 4, § 53 (Smith-Hurd 1979)
Indiana:	Ind.Code § 29 (1976) Ind.Code Ann. § 29 (Burns 1978) Ind.Code Ann. § 29 (West 1977)
Iowa:	Iowa Code § 72.3 (1979) Iowa Code Ann. § 72.3 (West 1980)
Kansas:	Kan.Stat.Ann. § 47 (1980) Kan. Civ.Proc.Code Ann. § 299 (Vernon 1970)
Kentucky:	Ky.Rev.Stat. § 222 (1979) Ky.Rev.Stat.Ann. § 222 (Baldwin 1980) Ky.Rev.Stat.Ann. § 222 (Bobbs-Merrill 1978)
Louisiana:	La.Rev.Stat.Ann. § 110 (West 1980) La.Code Crim.Proc.Ann. art. 3 (West 1980)
Maine:	Me.Rev.Stat.Ann. tit. 8, § 627 (1969)
Maryland:	Md.Fam.Law Code Ann. § 40 (1980)
Massachusetts:	Mass.Gen.Laws Ann. ch. 10, § 598 (West 1980) Mass.Ann.Laws ch. 10, § 598 (Michie/Law. Co-op.1979)
Michigan:	Mich.Comp.Laws § 2.1 (1978) Mich.Comp.Laws Ann. § 2.1 (1980) Mich.Stat.Ann. § 2.1 (1981)
Minnesota:	Minn.Stat. § 3678 (1980) Minn.Stat.Ann. § 3678 (1979)
Mississippi:	Miss.Code Ann. § 123 (1970)
Missouri:	Mo.Rev.Stat. § 48 (1979) Mo.Ann.Stat. § 48 (1981)
Montana:	Mont.Code Ann. § 1.23 (1982)
Nebraska:	Neb.Rev.Stat. § 97 (1979)
Nevada:	Nev.Rev.Stat. § 990 (1969)
New Hampshire:	N.H.Rev.Stat.Ann. § 538 (1980)
New Jersey:	N.J.Rev.Stat. § 50 (1980) N.J.Stat.Ann. § 50 (1979)
New Mexico:	N.M.Stat.Ann. § 717 (1979)
New York:	N.Y.Crim.Proc.Law § 150 (McKinney 1979) N.Y.Crim.Proc.Law § 150 (Consol.1980)

North Carolina:	N.C.Gen.Stat. § 373 (1979)
Ohio:	Ohio Rev.Code Ann. § 434.2 (Page 1979)
	Ohio Rev.Code Ann. § 434.2 (Baldwin 1980)
Oklahoma:	Okla.Stat. tit. 5, § 12 (1982)
	Okla.Stat.Ann. tit. 5, § 12 (West 1980)
Oregon:	Or.Rev.Stat. § 3636 (1980)
Pennsylvania:	12 Pa.Cons.Stat. § 578.9 (1979)
	12 Pa.Cons.Stat.Ann. § 578.9 (1980)
	Pa.Stat.Ann. tit. 12, § 578.9 (1979)
Puerto Rico:	P.R.Laws Ann. tit. 25, § 299 (1980)
Rhode Island:	R.I.Gen.Laws § 257 (1981)
South Carolina:	S.C.Code Ann. § 266 (Law.Co-op.1980)
South Dakota:	S.D.Codified Laws Ann. § 43 (1979)
	S.D.Comp.Laws Ann. § 43 (1980)
Tennessee:	Tenn.Code Ann. § 343 (1980)
Texas:	Tex.Penal Code Ann. § 777 (Vernon 1980)
Utah:	Utah Code Ann. § 1888 (1979)
Vermont:	Vt.Stat.Ann. tit. 3, § 26 (1978)
Virgin Islands:	V.I.Code Ann. tit. 9 (1979)
Virginia:	Va.Code § 345 (1979)
Washington:	Wash.Rev.Code § 2356 (1978)
	Wash.Rev.Code Ann. § 2356 (1980)
West Virginia:	W.Va.Code § 377 (1979)
Wisconsin:	Wis.Stat. § 7 (1980)
	Wis.Stat.Ann. § 7 (West 1979)
Wyoming:	Wyo.Stat. § 5656 (1980)

Appendix C

Bibliography on Legislative Analysis and Drafting

Allen, "Symbolic Logic: A Razor-Edged Tool for Drafting and Interpreting Legal Documents," 66 *Yale Law Journal* 833 (1957).

American Bar Association, Law Student Division, *Guide to Legislative Research and Drafting* (1979).

Anderson, "The Intention of the Framers: A Note on Constitutional Interpretation," 49 *Am.Pol.Sci.Rev.* 340 (1955).

Bishin, "The Law Finders: An Essay in Statutory Interpretation," 38 *Southern California Law Review* 1 (1965).

Block, *Effective Legal Writing* (1981).

Brand & White, *Legal Writing: The Strategy of Persuasion* (1976).

Broussard, "Punctuation of Statutes," 24 *Oregon Law Review* 157, 170 (1945).

Bruncken, "Interpretation of Written Law," 25 *Yale Law Journal* 129 (1915).

Chafee, "The Disorderly Conduct of Words," 41 *Columbia Law Review* 381 (1941).

Charrow, *What is Plain English, Anyway?* Document Design Center, American Institutes for Research (Dec. 1979).

Clark, "Special Problems in Drafting and Interpreting Procedural Codes and Rules," 3 *Vanderbilt Law Review* 493 (1950).

Cohen, "Judicial 'Legisputation' and the Dimensions of Legislative Meaning," 36 *Indiana Law Journal* 414 (1961).

Cohen, *Materials and Problems on Legislation* (2nd edition, 1967).

Cook, *Legal Drafting* (rev. ed. 1951).

Corry, "Administrative Law and the Interpretation of Statutes," 1 *University of Toronto Law Journal* 286 (1936).

Corry, "The Use of Legislative History in the Interpretation of Statutes," 32 *Canadian Bar Review* 624 (1954).

Craies, *A Treatise on Statute Law* (3rd ed. 1923).

Crawford, *The Construction of Statutes* (1940).

Cross, *Statutory Interpretation* (1976).

Curtis, "A Better Theory of Legal Interpretations," 3 *Vanderbilt Law Review* 407 (1950).

Davies, *Legislative Law and Process in a Nutshell* (1975).

Dernbach & Singleton, *A Practical Guide to Legal Writing and Legal Method* (1981).

de Sloovère, *Cases on Interpretation of Statutes* (1931).

de Sloovère, "Preliminary Questions in Statutory Interpretation," 9 *New York University Law Review* 407 (1932).

de Sloovère, "Steps in the Process of Interpreting Statutes," 10 *New York University Law Quarterly Review* 1 (1932).

de Sloovère, "The Equity and Reason of a Statute," 21 *Cornell Law Quarterly* 591 (1936).

de Sloovère, "The Functions of Judge and Jury in the Interpretation of Statutes," 46 *Harvard Law Review* 1061 (1933).

Dickerson, *The Fundamentals of Legal Drafting* (1965).

Dickerson, *Legislative Drafting* (1954).

Dickerson, *Materials on Legal Drafting* (1981).

Dreidger, *The Composition of Legislation—Legislative Forms and Precedents,* 2nd Ed. (1976).

Emerson & Fuller, "How to Find and Use Federal Legislative Materials," 51 *West Virginia Law Quarterly* 169 (1949).

Felsenfeld & Siegel, *Writing Contracts in Plain English* (1981).

Flesch, *The Art of Readable Writing* (1949).

Finley, "Crystal Gazing: The Problem of Legislative History," 45 *American Bar Association Journal* 1281 (1959).

Fordham & Leach, "Interpretation of Statutes in Derogation of the Common Law," 3 *Vanderbilt Law Review* 438 (1950).

Frank, "Words and Music: Some Remarks on Statutory Construction," 47 *Columbia Law Review* 1259 (1947).

Frankfurter, "Forward to a Symposium on Statutory Construction," 3 *Vanderbilt Law Review* 365 (1950).

Frankfurter "Some Reflections on the Reading of Statutes," 47 *Columbia Law Review* 527 (1947).

Freeman, *The Grammatical Lawyer* (1979).

French, B., "Council of the District of Columbia Legislative Drafting Manual, Revised Edition," 25 *Howard Law Journal* 731 (1982).

Freund, "Interpretation of Statutes," 65 *University of Pennsylvania Law Review* 207 (1917).

Freund, "The Use of Indefinite Terms in Statutes," 30 *Yale Law Journal* 437 (1921).

Gopen, *Writing from a Legal Perspective* (1981).

Holmes, "The Theory of Legal Interpretation," 12 *Harvard Law Review* 417 (1899).

Horack, "Cooperative Action for Improved Statutory Interpretation," 3 *Vanderbilt Law Review* 382 (1950).

Horack, "In the Name of Legislative Intention," 38 *West Virginia Law Quarterly* 119 (1932).

Horack, "The Disintegration of Statutory Construction," 24 *Indiana Law Journal* 335 (1949).

Jackson, "The Meaning of Statutes: What Congress Says or What the Court Says," 34 *American Bar Association Journal* 535 (1948).

Johnstone, "An Evaluation of the Rules of Statutory Interpretation," 3 *Kansas Law Review* 1 (1954).

Jones, "The Statutory Doubts and Legislative Intention," 40 *Columbia Law Review* 957 (1940).

Jones, "The Plain Meaning Rule and Extrinsic Aids in Interpretation of Federal Statutes," 25 *Washington University Law Quarterly* 2 (1939).

Landis, "A Note on Statutory Interpretation," 43 *Harvard Law Review* 886 (1930).

Lavery, "Punctuation in the Law," 9 *American Bar Association Journal* 225 (1923).

Llewellyn, "Remarks on the Theory of Appellate Decision and the Rules or Canons About How Statutes are to be Construed," 3 *Vanderbilt Law Review* 395 (1950).

Loyd, "The Equity of a Statute," 58 *University of Pennsylvania Law Review* 76 (1909).

MacCallum, "Legislative Intent," 75 *Yale Law Journal* 754 (1966).

Macdonald, "The Position of Statutory Construction in Present Day Law Practice," 3 *Vanderbilt Law Review* 369 (1950).

Maxwell, *Interpretation of Statutes* (7th ed. 1929).

Mellinkoff, *Legal Writing: Sense & Nonsense* (1982).

Mellinkoff, *The Language of the Law* (1963).

Miller, "Statutory Language and the Purposive Use of Ambiguity," 42 *Virginia Law Review* 23 (1956).

Moffat, "The Legislative Process," 24 *Cornell Law Quarterly* 223 (1939).

Nathanson, "Administrative Discretion in the Interpretation of Statutes," 3 *Vanderbilt Law Review* 470 (1950).

National Conference of Commissioners on Uniform State Laws, *Drafting Rules for Writing Uniform or Model Acts* (1965).

Newman, "How Courts Interpret Regulations," 35 *California Law Review* 509 (1947).

Note, "Administrative Tribunals, Judicial Review of Administrative Interpretations of Statutory Provisions: Recent Federal Developments," 47 *Michigan Law Review* 675 (1949).

Note, "A Note on Statutory Interpretation," 43 *Harvard Law Review* 886 (1930).

Note, "And/Or: Its Use and Abuse," 42 *West Virginia Law Quarterly* 235 (1936).

Note, "Bill-Drafting Services in Congress and the State Legislatures," 65 *Harvard Law Review* 441 (1952).

Note, "Due Process Requirements of Definiteness in Statutes," 62 *Harvard Law Review* 77 (1948).

Note, "In Defense of And/Or," 45 *Yale Law Journal* 918 (1936).

Note, "Nonlegislative Intent as an Aid to Statutory Interpretation," 49 *Columbia Law Review* 676 (1949).

Note, "The Supreme Court on Administrative Construction as a Guide in Interpretation of Statutes," 40 *Harvard Law Review* 469 (1927).

Note, "Use and Interpretation of 'And/Or,' " 11 *Wisconsin Law Review* 441 (1936).

Nutting, "The Ambiguity of Unambiguous Statutes," 24 *Minnesota Law Review* 509 (1940).

Nutting, "The Perils of Punctuation," 53 *American Bar Association Journal* 1072 (Nov. 1967).

Nutting, "The Relevance of Legislative Intention Established by Extrinsic Evidence," 20 *Boston University Law Review* 601 (1940).

Office of the Federal Register, *Document Drafting Handbook* (1980).

Ogden & Richards, *The Meaning of Meaning* (3rd ed. 1930).

Payne, "The Intention of the Legislature in the Interpretation of Statutes," 9 *Current Legal Problems* 96 (1956).

Phelps, "Factors Influencing Judges in Interpreting Statutes," 3 *Vanderbilt Law Review* 456 (1950).

Phelps, "What is a Question of Law?" 18 *University of Cincinnati Law Review* 259 (1949).

Plucknett, *Statutes and their Interpretation in the First Half of the Fourteenth Century* (1922).

Pound, "Common Law and Legislation," 21 *Harvard Law Review* 383 (1908).

Pound, "Spurious Interpretation," 7 *Columbia Law Review* 379 (1907).

Quarles, "Some Statutory Construction Problems and Approaches in Criminal Law," 3 *Vanderbilt Law Review* 531 (1950).

Radin, "A Short Way With Statutes," 56 *Harvard Law Review* 388 (1942).

Radin, "Realism in Statutory Construction and Elsewhere," 23 *California Law Review* 156 (1935).

Radin, "Statutory Interpretation," 43 *Harvard Law Review* 863 (1930).

Read, MacDonald, Fordham & Pierce, *Materials on Legislation* (1973).

Sanders & Wade, "Legal Writings on Statutory Construction," 3 *Vanderbilt Law Review* 569 (1950).

Scott, "The Judicial Power to Apply Statutes to Subjects to which they were not Intended to be Applied," 14 *Temple Law Quarterly* 318 (1940).

Silving, "A Plea for a Law of Interpretation," 98 *University of Pennsylvania Law Review* 499 (1950).

Squires & Rombauer, *Legal Writing in a Nutshell* (1982).

Strunk & White, *The Elements of Style,* 3rd Ed. (1979).

Sutherland, *Statutory Construction,* 4th Edition, D. Sands, editor, five volumes (1972).

Sutton, "The Use of 'Shall' in Statutes," 4 *John Marshall Law Quarterly* 204 (1938).

Thomas, "Statutory Construction When Legislation Viewed as a Legal Institution," 3 *Harvard Journal of Legislation* 191 (1965–66).

Tunks, "Assigning Legislative Meaning: A New Battle," 37 *Iowa Law Review* 372 (1952).

Wasby, "Legislative Materials as an Aid to Statutory Interpretation," 12 *J.Pub.Law* 264 (1964).

Weihofen, *Legal Writing Style,* 2d Ed. (1980).

White, *The Legal Imagination: Studies in the Nature of Legal Thought and Expression* (1973).

Williams, "Expressio Unius Est Exclusio Alterius," 15 *Marquette Law Review* 191 (1931).

Williams, "Language and the Law," 62 *Law Quarterly Review* 387 (1946).

Willis, "Statute Interpretation in a Nutshell," 16 *Canadian Bar Review* 1 (1938).

Witherspoon, "Administrative Discretion to Determine Statutory Meaning: 'The Middle Road,' " 40 *Texas Law Review* 751 (1962).

Witherspoon, "The Essential Focus of Statutory Interpretation," 36 *Indiana Law Journal* 423 (1961).

Wydick, *Plain English for Lawyers* (1979).

Zinn, *How Our Laws are Made* (1961).

Index

A

A, 185
Absurd results, 81
Active verbs, 182
Active voice, 180
Adjective forms, 185
Administrative agency, 7, 39, 63, 78, 101, 121, 155, 171
Administrative costs of a new law, 164
Administrative decisions, 39, 78, 98
Administrative provisions of a new law, 170
Administrative regulations, 7, 39, 65, 98, 171
Adverb, 185
Advocacy, 63, 97, 99
Agency, administrative 7, 39, 63, 78, 101, 121, 155, 171

Ali, 184
ALR, 194
Ambiguity, 3, 13, 16, 41, 50, 55, 75, 89, 111, 118, 136, 152, 174, 183
Amendments, 38, 40, 102, 108, 112, 118, 166, 169, 195
American Law Institute, 164
American Law Reports, 194
Analysis in a memorandum of law, 47, 64
Analysis in general, 1, 46, 64
And, 50, 140, 184
And/or, 184
Annotated code, 39, 43, 193, 197
Annotations, 194
Any, 184, 185
Appellate brief, 63
Appendix, 64, 66
Art, terms of, 94, 190
Article, 185

Imperative mood, 176, 179
Implied language, 50, 133, 137
In pari materia, 93
Index to Legal Periodicals, 41, 194
Indicative mood, 176, 179
Information Handling Service, 196
Intent of legislature, 10, 15, 77, 109, 126, 137, 145, 152
Interoffice memorandum of law, 47, 62
Interpretation, 3
Interviewing, 47
Investigating committee, 101
Investigation, 47
Issues, 47, 55, 64
It, 183

J

Journals,
  Law (legal periodicals), 37, 41, 164, 194, 196
  Legislative, 196
Judicial legislation, 6
Judicial review, 152
Judiciary, 152

L

Language, 14, 15, 83, 95, 112, 133, 186
Law reviews, 37, 41, 164, 194, 196
Law Revision Commission, 101, 123, 197
Legal analysis, 1, 46, 64
Legal issues, 47, 55, 64
Legal memorandum, 47, 62
Legal periodicals, 37, 41, 164, 194, 196
Legal research, 37, 40, 163, 193
Legal Resource Index, 41, 194
Legislative committee, 4, 20, 38, 78, 99, 101, 121, 196
Legislative committee reports, 38, 102, 108, 121, 196

Legislative counsel, 122
Legislative drafting, 16, 20, 84, 111, 161
Legislative drafting office, 122
Legislative hearings, 102, 108, 122, 196
Legislative history, 4, 5, 37, 38, 65, 76, 78, 86, 91, 97ff, 136, 165, 195ff
Legislative intent, 10, 15, 77, 109, 126, 137, 145, 152
Legislative journals, 196
Legislative process, 15
Legislative purpose, 36, 76, 99, 109, 126, 127, 130, 136, 162, 166
Legislative services, 40, 123, 197
Legislature, 6, 7, 10, 15, 18, 38, 100
Letters, 62, 71
Liberal interpretation, 19, 125
Library, depository, 121
Lists, 46, 49, 90, 172
Literal interpretation, 14, 127
Long title, 165
Loose leaf services, 40, 123, 194

M

Majority report, 102, 103
Mandatory language, 133
May, 133, 136, 180
Meaning, 8, 15, 17, 18
Means and includes, 175
Memorandum of law, 47, 62
Microfiche, 122, 196
Minority reports, 102, 103
Mischief rule, 19, 35, 76, 91, 94, 99, 126, 131, 136, 137
Modifiers, 49, 139
Monthly Catalog of U.S. Documents, 122, 196
Mood, 176, 179
Motives, 113
Must, 133

V

Vague language, 11, 15, 110, 126
Verb tense, 176, 179
Vested rights, 147
Voice, 180

W

Writing legislation, 16, 20, 84, 111, 161

†